CALIFORNIA
America's First New England

by
Dr. Catherine Millard

© Copyright 2010

Christian Heritage Ministries®
P.O. Box 797
Springfield, Virginia 22150
703-455-0333
www.christianheritagemins.org
www.christianheritagetours.org

ISBN No: 978-0-692-01131-7
Library of Congress Catalog Card No: 2010913049

Published by: Christian Heritage Ministries®

Printed in the United States of America

*Scripture quotations taken from the 1611 King James translation of the Holy
Bible, from the original tongues.*

Front Cover: View of San Francisco, formerly Yerba Buena, in 1846-7.
Signed: Gen. M.G. Vallejo, and George Hyde,
First Alcalde of San Francisco, 1846-7.

CALIFORNIA
AMERICA'S FIRST NEW ENGLAND

Table of Contents

DEDICATION

To the Four California Founders – pioneer
missionaries, whose work and foundations
continue – though they "rest from their
labors, their works do follow them."

Preface

"Let There be Light"

Hymn of the University of California*

Father of Lights, with whom no
change nor shadow of return,
Hath been or ever star could range,
Or sun begin to burn. Amen.

O Thou, from whom all pow'r
proceeds, to bless Thy worlds with birth,
Bestow on us the Light that leads
To fuller life on earth:

The truth that maketh not ashamed,
The love that maketh one,
The will to lift Thy weak and maimed
So shall Thy will be done.

And all the praise to Thee be given
For all Thy gifts to us:
Let there be Light in earth as heaven,
O Light most glorious![1]

*Words by Charles Mills Gayley, 1904.
  Tule: "St. Anne" by Watts-Croft.

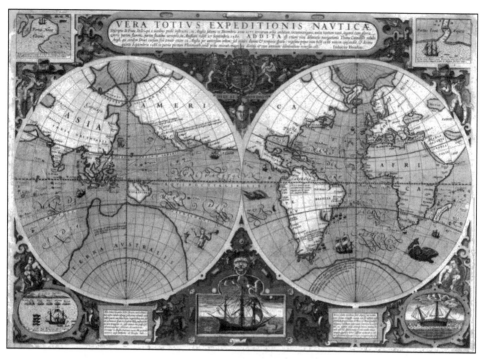

Famed Judocus Hondius, circa 1595 map of Sir Francis Drake's circumnavigation of the world.

Chaplain Fletcher "The World Encompassed by Sir Francis Drake

Introduction

San Francisco, California, is best remembered for the 1849 Gold Rush, with its fevered lust for gain and monetary success.

However, San Francisco's first love can be traced to *June* 1579 when Sir Francis Drake sailed into her beautiful harbor on the **Golden Hinde**, disembarking to conduct the first Protestant Christian worship service upon her shores. The event took place twenty-eight years before the first permanent Protestant Christian settlement was established in Jamestown, Virginia, on the eastern shores of America.

To quote the eminent, scholarly historian, named "dean of California historians:"

> The first New England did not begin at Jamestown or at Plymouth Rock, nor did it border on the Atlantic Ocean. It is claimed for *Alta California* and the North Pacific coast, and it dates a generation prior to the settlement of the Virginia colony, many years before the Pilgrim Fathers brought the *Mayflower* to anchor off the coast of Massachusetts. It was on a June day in 1579...that Drake sailed the *Golden Hinde* into "a conuenient and fit harborough" long believed to be what is known as Drake's Bay, some thirty miles north of the Golden Gate. There he took formal possession of the land for Queen Elizabeth, naming it **Nova** (New) **Albion.**[1]

Sir Francis Drake. Attributed to Judocus Hondius and reworked by George Vertue.

CHAPTER I

The First New England
"Nova Albion"

This unprecedented Californian "first" is vividly described in *The World Encompassed by Sir Francis Drake,* by his chaplain, Francis Fletcher. Published in London in 1628, the fascinating story of Drake's arrival at San Francisco Bay on June 17, 1579; his friendly encounter with the Indians; their great *Hioh*, or King freely bestowing upon him the full title and ownership of California; and Drake's setting up "a brasse plate" claiming the land for Queen Elizabeth I, begins thus:

> Ever since **Almighty God** commanded Adam to subdue the earth, there have not wanted, in all ages, some heroical spirits, which in obedience to that high mandate, either from manifest reason alluring them, or by secret instinct enforcing them thereunto, have expended their wealth, employed their times, and adventured their persons, to find out the true circuit thereof.

> Of these, some have endeavoured to effect this their purpose, by conclusion and consequence, drawn from the proportion of higher circles, to this nethermost globe, being the center of the rest. Others, not content with school points, and such demonstrations (for that a small error in the beginning, grows in the progress to a great inconvenience) have added thereunto their own history and experience. All of them in reason have deserved great commendation of their own ages, and purchased a just renown with all posterity. For if a surveyor of some few Lordships, whereof the bounds and limits were before known, worthily deserve his reward, not only for his travel, but for his skill also, in measuring the whole and every part thereof: how much more, above comparison are their famous travels by all means possible to be eternalized, who have bestowed their studies and endeavor, to survey and measure this globe almost unmeasurable? Neither is here that difference to be objected, which of private possessions is of value: whose land survey you? Foreasmuch as the **main ocean by right** is **the Lord's** alone, and by nature left free, for all men to deal withal, as very sufficient for all men's use, and large enough for all men's industry. And therefore that valiant enterprise, accompanied with happy success, which that right rare and thrice worthy *Captain Francis Drake* achieved, in first turning up a furrow about the whole world, does not only over-match the ancient Argonautes, but also outreaches in many respects, that noble mariner, Magellanus,

Francis Drake crowned king by the Great Hioh.
From an old Engraving. Artist Unknown.

and by far surpasses his crowned victory. But hereof let posterity judge.

Francis Drake's Encounter with the Indians - His worship of Almighty God on the Shore

Sir Francis Drake's encounter with the Indians and his worship of **Almighty God** on the shores of what is now San Francisco, continues in this unique and exciting vein:

…Our General with his company, in the presence of those strangers, fell to prayer: and by signs in lifting up our eyes and hands to heaven, signified unto them, that **God whom we did serve**, and whom they ought to worship, was above: beseeching God if it were His good pleasure, to open by some means their blinded eyes; that they might in due time be called to the knowledge of Him, the **true and everliving God, and of Jesus Christ**, whom He hath sent, the salvation of the gentiles. In the time of which prayers, singing of **Psalms**, and reading of certain chapters in **the Bible**, they sat very attentively, and observing the end at every pause, with one voice still cried – Oh, greatly rejoicing in our exercises. Yea, they took such pleasure in our singing of **Psalms,** that whensoever they resorted to us, their first request was commonly this, *"Gnaah,"* by which they intreated that we would sing.

…they made signs to **our General** to have him sit down; unto whom both the king and divers others made several orations…that he would **take the Province and kingdom** into his hand, and become the king and patron: making signs that they would **resign unto him their right and title in the whole land**, and become vassals in themselves and their posterities:…

These things being so freely offered, our General thought not meet to reject or refuse the same: both for that he would not give them any cause of mistrust, or disliking of, him (that being the only place, wherein at this present, we were of necessity enforced to seek relief of many things), and chiefly, for that he knew not to what good end **God has brought this to pass**, or what honour and profit it might bring to our country in time to come…

Francis Drake's meeting with the great Hioh.
From Theodore de Bry, Historia Americae, Part VIII, 1599.

This country our General named *ALBION*, and that for two causes: the one in respect of the white banks and cliffs which lie *toward* the sea: the other, that it might have some affinity, even in name only, with our own country, which was sometime so called.

Before we went from thence, our General caused to be set up, a monument of our being there; as also of her majesties and successors right and title to that kingdome, namely, **a plate of brasse**, fast nailed to a great and **firme post**; whereon is engraven her ~Queen~ graces name, and the day and yeare of our arrival there, and of the *Elizabeth* free giving up, of the Province and kingdome, both by the king and people, into her majesties hands: together with her highnesse picture, and armes in a piece of sixpence current English monie, shewing itselfe by a hole made of purpose through the plate: underneath was likewise engraven the name of our Generall, etc.

THE VVORLD
Encompaſſed

By
Sir FRANCIS DRAKE,

Being his next voyage to that to *Nombre de Dios* formerly imprinted;

Carefully collected out of the notes of Maſter FRANCIS FLETCHER *Preacher in this imployment, and diuers others his followers in the ſame* :

Offered now at laſt to publique view, both for the honour of the actor, but eſpecially for the ſtirring vp of *heroick ſpirits,* to benefit their Countrie, and eternize their names by like noble attempts.

LONDON,
Printed for NICHOLAS BOVRNE
and are to be ſold at his ſhop at the
Royall Exchange. 1628.

Original title page of The World Encompassed by Sir Francis Drake, 1628

CHAPTER II

Drake's Plate of Brass Discovered - 1937

A 1937 **California Historical Society** publication entitled, *Drake's Plate of Brass – Evidence of his visit to California in 1579*, informs readers of the amazing discovery of Francis Drake's original brass plate, 357 years later!

On April 6, 1937, Herbert E. Bolton, Professor of American History and Director of the Rare Book and Manuscript - **Bancroft Library** of the **University of California**, delivered a riveting speech before the California Historical Society. This occurred at the Sir Francis Drake Hotel in San Francisco, on the occasion announcing the Drake Plate discovery. It is hereunder excerpted:

> One of the world's long-lost historical treasures apparently has been found! Three hundred and fifty-seven years ago, Francis Drake, on the *Golden Hinde* made his famous voyage round the world, the first accomplished by any Englishman. On June 17, 1579, while on the way to the Orient, he anchored in a "conuenient and fit harborough" on the California coast and there reconditioned his ship. Before he left he nailed to a **"firme post"** a **brass plate** bearing an inscription. It was a bold notice to all the world that for Queen Elizabeth of England, he had taken possession of the country, which he called *New Albion*. He gave it this name, be-cause the white cliffs along the coast reminded him of the chalk cliffs of England, from which the Romans gave the name of Albion to that island.
>
> These facts are recorded in the well-known narratives of Drake's voyage. But from that day to this – a period of more than three and one-half centuries – **the plate** has not been seen by any white man, so far as records show. Nor has anybody known the exact words with which Drake issued his challenge to the world. But the plate, it seems, has been found. England can now quote the very phrases with which her most celebrated navigator proclaimed Elizabeth's title to California. The relic tallies in a most astonish-ing way with the description in the narrative by Chaplain Francis Fletcher, who was with Drake, who doubtless saw the plate, and who witnessed its nailing to the **"firme post,"** or to the "faire great poste," as it was called. The relic is of **solid brass**, about five inches wide and eight inches long, and an eighth of an inch thick. It was picked up by Beryle Shinn in the summer of 1936 in Marin County not far from San Rafael. After keeping it some six months

Francis Drake's "Plate of Brasse" — Discovered in 1937.

without an inkling of its unique character, he brought it to me early in February, 1937, and I told him what I thought it was...The sixpence was not found with the plate and is still missing. (Perhaps I ought to say that Mr. Shinn was not one of my students and had little or no knowledge of the Drake voyage until he talked with me). The authenticity of the tablet seems to me beyond all reasonable doubt. On this assumption, its discovery is one of the most sensational in all California history.

With a view to announcing the event through the appropriate channel, and of obtaining the financial assistance necessary to acquire the precious relic for the University of California, I turned to **Allen L. Chickering, President** of the **California Historical Society**, who in times past has generously responded to more than one similar appeal. With his accustomed energy and enthusiasm in the cause of California history, he raised the necessary funds, from the donors whose names are elsewhere given, joined me in negotiations with Mr. Shinn, and acquired the relic. In fairness to Mr. Shinn, it should be said that, as soon as he learned of its significance, his chief interest in the plate was to have it preserved for the public, and he never asked, nor would he discuss a price for it. (This fact has, of course, an important bearing on the question of the genuineness of the plate). The sum paid was suggested by Mr. Chickering, and was regarded by him and his associates as merely a suitable reward for generous cooperation in releasing the plate in order that it might go to the University...

It is only through the accident that Mr. Shinn came to me that I have this honor. My aim in this brief sketch is simply to recall the circumstances under which Drake took possession of *New Albion*, and to present the convincing evidence of the genuineness of the plate which has been discovered...

In the fall of 1577 he sailed from England with five ships bound for the Orient. Drake's plan was to continue across the Pacific to the Moluccas, but it was now too late to catch the favorable winds...He could not risk the vessel so heavily laden for so long a voyage at the wrong season of the year. He dared not return through the Strait of Magellan, for the Spaniards would be sure to lie in wait for him there...When the proper time arrived, he coasted south, looking for a harbor in which to recondition the *Golden Hinde* before striking across the Pacific on the long, hard voyage.

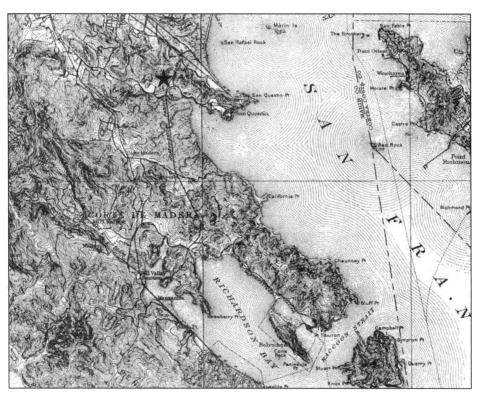

The Star indicates where the Plate of Brass was found.
Reproduced from U.S. Topographic Map.

On the way he anchored in an unsatisfactory inlet...Thence he continued down the coast and in "38 deg. 30. min....fell with a conuenient and fit harborough, and June 17. came to anchor therein," remaining till July 23. Drake's dates of course were Old Style...

The discovery of the **"plate of brasse"** lends fresh interest to the scene enacted that summer of 1579 on the California coast...

The Indians brought to the Commander presents "in such sort, as if they had appeared before a god indeed." The women were so worshipful that when they came to camp and beheld the armor-covered, bearded and fair-haired visitors, they "used unnatural violence against themselves, crying and shrieking piteously, tearing their flesh with their nailes from their cheeks, in a monstrous manner, the blood streaming downe along their brests; besides despoiling the upper parts of their bodies, of those single coverings they formerly had, and holding their hands above their heads, that they might not rescue their brests from harme, they would with furie cast themselves upon the ground," dashing their naked bodies upon "hard stones, knobbly hillocks, stocks of wood, and pricking bushes."

...On June 26 the great *Hioh* himself appeared on the hilltop, "a man of goodly stature and comely personage, attended with his guard, of about 100. tall and warlike men...In the forefront came a man of large body and goodly aspect, bearing the septre or royall mace...Whereupon hanged two crownes...with three chaines of a marvelous length...The crownes were made of knitworke, wrought upon most curiously with feathers of divers colours, very artificially placed, and of a formall fashion." The chains were equally marvelous. They appeared to be "of a bony substance: every linke or part thereof being very little, thinne, most finely burnished, with a hole pierced through the middest. The number of linkes going to make one chaine," says Fletcher, "is in a manner infinite."

...With impassioned eloquence and exquisite ceremonial, we are told, the *Hioh* and his retainers begged the General to accept the country and become its ruler. The words of Chaplain Fletcher here are pertinent to the sequel: "After that they had satisfied or rather tired themselves in this manner, says Fletcher, **"they made signes to our Generall** to have him sit down; unto whom both **the**

"The Golden Hinde", Sir Francis Drake's Ship, from the Judocus Hondius, circa 1595 Map.

king and divers others made several orations, or indeed, if wee had understood them, supplications, **that hee would take the Province and kingdome into his hand,** and become their king and patron: making signes that they would **resigne unto him their right and title to the whole land**, and become vassals in themselves and their posterities." And, "that they might make us indeed believe that it was their true meaning and intent, the king himselfe, with all the rest, with one consent and with great reverence, joyfully singing a song, set the crowne upon his head; inriched his necke with all their chaines; and...honoured him by the name of *Hyoh*: Adding thereunto (as it might seeme) a song and a dance of triumph; because they were not onely visited of the gods (for so they still judged us to be), but the great and chiefe god was now become their god, their king and patron, and themselves were become the onely happie and blessed people in all the world."

...And so, says the Chaplain, "These things" – California and the Crown – "being so freely offered, our Generall thought not meet to reject or refuse the same: both for that he would not give them any cause of mistrust, or disliking of him (that being the onely place, wherein at this present, we were of necessitie inforced to seeke reliefe of many things) and chiefely, for that he knew not to what good end had brought this to passe, or what honour and profit it might bring to our countrie in time to come. Wherefore, in the name and to the use of her most excellent majesty, he tooke the sceptre, crowne and dignity, of the sayd countrie into his hand; wishing nothing more, than that it had layen so fitly for her majesty to enjoy, as it was now her proper owne, and that the riches and treasures thereof...might with as great conveniency be transported to the enriching of the kingdome here at home, (Fletcher was writing in England) as it is in plenty to be attained there: and especially, that so tractable and loving a people, as they showed themselves to be, might have meanes to have manifested their most willing obedience the more unto her, and by her meanes, as a mother and nurse of the **Church of Christ**, might by the **preaching of the Gospell**, be brought to the right knowledge and obedience of the true and everliving God."

THE

Plate of Brass

EVIDENCE OF THE VISIT OF

Francis Drake

TO CALIFORNIA IN THE YEAR

1579

CALIFORNIA HISTORICAL SOCIETY

Title Page of The Plate of Brass, Evidence of the Visit of Francis Drake to California in the Year 1579, publication.

Francis Drake crowned
great *Hioh* of California

Thus was Drake crowned great *Hioh* of California. He called the country *Nova Albion,* or New Albion, "and that for two causes," says the Chaplain, "the one in respect of the white bancks and cliffs, which lie toward the sea: the other, that it might have some affinities, even in name also, with our owne country, which was sometime so called."

As has been stated above, Fletcher is our chief source of information for details regarding events at the "conuenient and fit harborough."

...No picture of the plate is known to exist. Only one recourse remained – to find the plate. Here it is! Recovered at last after a lapse of 357 years! Behold, Drake's plate – **the plate of brasse**! California's choicest archaeological treasure! And here is what the inscription says:

BEE IT KNOWNE VNTO ALL MEN BY THESE
PRESENTS
IVNE 17 1579

BY THE GRACE OF GOD AND IN THE NAME OF HERR
MAIESTY QUEEN ELIZABETH OF ENGLAND AND HERR
SVCCESSORS FOREVER I TAKE POSSESSION OF THIS
KINGDOME WHOSE KING AND PEOPLE FREELY RESIGNE
THEIR RIGHT AND TITLE IN THE WHOLE LAND VNTO HERR
MAIESTIES KEEPEING NOW NAMED BY ME AN TO BEE
KNOWNE VNTO ALL MEN AS NOVA ALBION

FRANCIS DRAKE

Hole for
silver
sixpence

So the plate, assuming its authenticity, completely vindicates Chaplain Fletcher. The phraseology of the inscription in nearly every particular is that of *The World Encompassed,* our fullest version of Fletcher's account.

1. The inscription claims *Nova Albion* for the Virgin Queen and her successors, just as the Chaplain says.
2. The plate is of **brass**, just as the Chaplain says.
3. Not the "province and people" but the "**province and kingdome**" and the "**right and title in the whole land**" were given up, just as the Chaplain says. .
4. They were granted not by a nameless nobody, but by "**king and people**" the great Hioh and his subjects, just as the Chaplain says.
5. Finally, there is **a hole** through the plate "**made of purpose**" to hold **the sixpence**, just as the Chaplain says.

Mr. Chickering obtained a **silver sixpence** bearing **Queen Elizabeth's picture** and it is a **perfect fit**. From that jagged window in the plate, after Drake departed, Queen Elizabeth looked majestically into the faces of the great *Hioh* and his people, and out upon fair California…Between the relic and the eye-witness records there is a spectacular and convincing harmony which no fraud would be likely to attain.

A few more remarks may be made regarding the plate. It is crudely made, fashioned as best it could be under the circumstances. This is one of the best testimonials to its genuineness. Approximately rectangular, even in shape it is irregular, one of its edges being slightly curved. At top and bottom there are generous notches through which to drive the spikes fastening it to the "**fair greate poste.**" The lettering is crude, made with a sharp tool, perhaps a cold chisel. One of the accounts says the letters were "scratched" on the plate, and all the curved lines look as though this in fact were the case. The words are unevenly spaced and the lines are not very straight. The surface of the plate is uneven, with pits or depressions in places, as though it had been hammered. The relic bears indications of having been long in contact with the soil, for when found, the incisions forming the letters were full of hard packed dirt.

The plate was found about a mile and a half west-northwest of San Quentin, near Cunningham Cement Works and Green Brae. The places here named are on the north shore of *Corte Madera Creek and Inlet,* which open on the east into the main *San Francisco Bay*. It is one of the most sheltered spots in the entire harbor. The plate was found near an outcropping of rocks on a high ridge about 500 feet from the water's edge. The hills near the bay are now nearly treeless, but farther inland the country is timbered.

The evidence furnished by the plate itself and the circumstances of its discovery leave little room to doubt its authenticity. The lettering and spelling of the inscription are in keeping with the period and with the Drake documents. The piece of brass on which the notice of possession was so crudely printed bears a marked resemblance to the plentiful brass-work on sixteenth century ships. In Drake's day, deck fittings were usually of bronze or brass. An experienced **sea-Captain** who examined the plate expressed the opinion that it might have been cut out of the **brass track of a gun-carriage**. This would account for the curved edge of the plaque, and perhaps for the pits. The square notches for the spikes are significant, for sixteenth century nails and spikes were customarily hand-wrought and were square.

If the Drake Plate is bogus, **the hoax** was perpetrated by someone who not only had studied *The World Encompassed* minutely, but who also had a knowledge of ship fittings and even of spikes. Anyone clever enough to have made a counterfeit tablet as convincing as the one just discovered, would have been clever enough to market it at an impressive figure. A fraudulent plaque might be expected to have a more skillfully executed hole for displaying the coin. For who, from the description, would imagine so crude and jagged an aperture through which to display the **image of the Queen?** Finally, since **Drake's Bay** has been so long regarded as the site of **Drake's landing**, a bogus tablet presumably would have been planted near that place, or, if the hoax were recent, perhaps near Bodega Bay, and not near *San Francisco Bay*, which has long been rejected as the site of Drake's landing place.

The exact location where the plate was found may, or may not have any bearing on the question of the identity of the harbor in which Drake beached his ship. In the matter of distance, it is near enough to fit any one of the three chief claimants – San Francisco Bay, Drake's Bay, or Bodega Bay. It is on the very shore of **San Francisco Bay**, some twenty-five miles air line from Drake's Bay and forty miles from Bodega Bay. **The plate** could easily have been **carried by Indians** from any one of those places to the spot where it was found. *The Great Hioh* might have worn it around his neck as an additional ornament. More likely, it was long regarded as an object of awe and veneration. In fact, one of the narratives states that even before Drake departed, the natives worshipped it **"as if it had bin god."** It is conceivable that investigation may prove that the plate was discovered in the very site where Drake nailed it to the "firme post," and that the beach at the foot of the hill was the very spot where he careened and repaired the *Golden Hinde.* In that case, we may prophesy, some day, there will arise on that commanding site, a fitting monument to one of the most dramatic episodes in California's history.

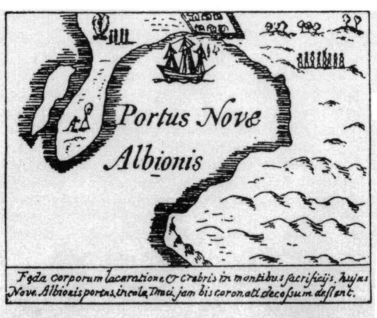

Feda corporum laceratione & crabris in montibus sacrificijs, hujus Nove Albionis portus, incola Traci, jam bis coron.all decossum dessent.

By horrible lacerations of their bodies and by frequent sacrifices in the mountains, the inhabitants of this part of New Albion deplore the departure of Drake now twice crowned.

Vignette from the Judocus Hondius circa 1595 map, showing the Portus Nove Albionis where Drake anchored.

Drake and California – The Finding of Evidence
of his Visit and its Implications

The same 1937 publication quotes **Chairman of the Publication Committee, California Historical Society**, Douglas S. Watson's detailed account of the discovery entitled: ***Drake and California – The Finding of Evidence of his Visit and its Implications***:

"…Today we possess startling and tangible proof: the brass plate that Francis Drake caused to be made and placed "upon a faire great poste." As notice to the world that he had taken possession of **New Albion** in the name of **Queen Elizabeth of England** and her successors. The finding this, the **rarest of Americana**, will doubtless result in endless discussion from which a new flood of literature will emerge. How it was found and where, may, at first glance, seem incidental, but the implications which will be drawn from the discovery are certain to have a bearing on the conclusions which future writers of California history will present.

A Sunday holiday late in June or early **July** of last year (**1936**) led the finder to Marin County. It was his initial visit to that section, and after roaming about the highways in his automobile, he drove south from San Rafael on the road leading to Greenbrae. Before reaching the east-west road which crosses that on which he was traveling and which joins San Quentin with Kingfield, one of the car's tires was punctured. Veering to the side of the road, he stopped his machine. The day was fine, the puncture could wait, for near at hand a picnic spot offered. A steep bluff rose from the roadside, but a way was found to reach its top. The ascent of a gully, and crawling beneath a "barbwire" fence, brought the picnicers to the spot. There, an extensive view presented itself. Toward the east lay *Point San Quentin*, with the forbidding walls of the State Prison, and the upper reaches of *San Francisco Bay*. To the southward, the bay shore curved and culminated in Bluff Point, the tip of the *Tiburon peninsula*, with Angel Island just beyond. Into the embayment between *Point San Quentin* and *Tiburon peninsula* a tidal estuary entered, which was the outlet for *Corte Madera Creek*, the small stream that rises in the heights of *Mount Tamalpais* to the west. Through a gap in the San Quentin ridge to the northeast, **San Francisco Bay** was again visible, likewise the entrance to *San Pablo Bay*; and on a clear day it is possible that the distant *Sierra Nevada* could be seen. The topography just described will doubtless be much studied in the future, for a careful scrutiny of its features may reveal clues which will lead to a solving of the problem of the location of the site of Drake's landing place.

February 28, 1937, in company with **Mr. Allen L. Chickering** and **Dr. Herbert E. Bolton**, the **finder of the brass plate, Mr. Beryle Shinn**, visited Marin County. He retraced the route he had followed six or more months previously. Finally, and after much difficulty, for he was unfamiliar with the countryside – in fact this was his second visit to Marin County – Shinn indicated that spot where the puncture had occurred, and the party climbed to the top of the steep bank.

'I found the plate by some rocks on the hillside,' said Shinn. 'We were rolling rocks down the hill. They were very brittle and they would break off easily. It was while I was picking up a rock that I noticed the plate lying on the ground. It was partly covered by a rock.'

Dr. Bolton asked, 'Was the plate covered by the rock? Before you picked up the rock, could the plate be seen?' To these questions Shinn replied, 'It could be seen. It was only partly covered by the rock.' Shinn explained that when he first saw the plate, he thought that it was iron, and because it was about the size to patch a hole in the inside of his automobile, he picked it up and carried it down to the car. For over a month he gave the black piece of metal no thought, when one day he decided to repair the automobile. While handling **the plate**, he noticed that it seemed to have **some inscription** on it. He showed it to a few of his friends, but none could make out what it was, until one of them deciphered the word **'Drake.'** Then it was suggested that Shinn show the plate to Dr. Bolton, of the University of California.

The suppressed excitement of the learned historian can well be imagined as he studied the plate's markings, and with unhurried care, unraveled what at first glance was a tangled mass of threadlike gravings on the brass. When he had finished, the message that no white man had seen for **three hundred and fifty-eight years** lay before him.

Here was something that all historians had clamored for; concrete **evidence of Drake's** activities in **California.** Dr. Bolton's immediate thought was, "How can this archeological relic be acquired and preserved for all time? For answer he turned to **Mr. Chickering,** who, besides being a friend of the Doctor's and an alumnus of the University of California, was **President of the California Historical Society**. Negotiations with the finder of the plate were begun, which Mr. Chickering successfully conducted, and a group of San Franciscans, all members of the California Historical Society, joined the Society's president in furnishing the necessary funds. These gentlemen, on behalf of the *California Historical Society* and themselves, have made a gift of the Drake plate to the University of California, and by the deed of gift have provided for its care and preservation.

The generosity and public spirit of these gentlemen cannot be too highly praised, nor should their names go unrecorded as deserving the sincere thanks of all English-speaking people.

Not one of those whose privilege it has been to examine the brass plate has doubted its genuineness. The two earliest accounts of Drake's voyage – 'The Famous Voyage,' included as an insert in the edition of **1589** of **Richard Hakluyt's** *The Prncipal Navigations, Voyages and Discoveries of the English Nation,* and *The World Encompassed,* published in **1628** from the 'notes of Master Francis Fletcher...and divers others his followers,' and with a dedication by the nephew of the circumnavigator who bore his distinguished name – both describe the setting up **a post** upon which **a plate**, asserting **English sovereignty**, was affixed. Says the **Hakluyt** version:

> At our departure hence our General set up a monument of our being there, as also of her Majesties right and title to the same, namely a plate, nailed upon a faire great poste, whereupon was engraven her Majesties name, the day and yeare of our arrival there, with the free giving up of the province and people unto her Majesties hands, together with her highness picture and armes, in a peece of sixe pence of current English money under the plate, where under was also written the name of our Generall.

The account printed in *The World Encompassed* is even more explicit:

> Before we went from thence, our Generall caused to be set up, a monument of our being there; as also of her majesties, and successors right and title to that kingdome, namely, a plate of brasse, fast nailed to a great and firme post; whereon is engraven her graces name, and the day and yeare of our arrival there, and of the free giving up of the province and kingdome, both by the king and people, into her majesties hands: together with her highnesse picture, and armes in a piece of sixpence current English monie, shewing it selfe by a hole made of purpose through the plate: underneath was likewise engraven the name of our Generall, &c.

Nothing is more convincing than the hole in the plate; and when an **Elizabethan sixpence** is inserted in the jagged points, seemingly provided especially to hold it, all doubt of the relic's authenticity vanishes.

Some may argue that the plate had been set up elsewhere, and had been brought to the spot where it was found; but when one familiar with the topography of the terrain where *Corte Madera Creek* enters **San Francisco Bay**, reads the Fletcher narrative as published by Hakluyt, and the version set forth in *The World Encompassed*, it is seemingly possible to distinguish all the landmarks mentioned.

A further argument may be advanced to substantiate the *Corte Madera Creek* site, now known as *Greenbrae*, as the location of Drake's stay in California. The celebrated vignette in the upper left-hand corner of the ***Hondius broadside map***, which has engaged the attention of many historians, since it purports to depict the scene of **Drake's landing,** can, with less torture than that to which it heretofore has been subjected, be made to fit the locale. The jutting peninsula of the ***Hondius map*** has more than a faint resemblance to the *Tiburon peninsula*, while the island lying at its side may be taken to be Angel Island. The anchorage of the ***Golden Hinde*** would then be the mouth of *Corte Madera Creek*, and the other enclosing arm protecting the "Portus" would be *Point San Quentin*. This possibility is offered, not as a solution, but as a suggestion...

Drake's position in the **history of America** today rests upon a firm foundation, and now that we have the evidence to support it, he can truly be regarded as **the first English-speaking settler in the western hemisphere**. His occupation of a portion of California, though temporary, antedates the Roanoke settlement of Sir Walter Raleigh by six years. Raleigh's occupation was likewise of an ephemeral nature, for the year after it was started the colonists returned to England, and the man who undertook their repatriation , and saw them safely back to the homeland was Drake, then Sir Francis, his knighthood being a part of the reward Queen Elizabeth bestowed upon him for his many daring exploits, including his discovery and occupation of *New Albion.*"

Drake's Plate of Brass Authenticated –
The Report on the Plate of Brass

In a further 1938, **California Historical Society** publication entitled, *Drake's Plate of Brass Authenticated – The Report on the Plate of Brass,* by **Colin G. Fink, Ph.D., D.Sc.,** Head of the Division of Electrochemistry, **Columbia University**, and **E.P. Polushkin,** Consulting **Metallurgical Engineer** (with Biographical note on Professor Fink by Joel H. Hildebrand, Ph.D., Professor of Chemistry, University of California) we read about the President of the California Historical Society, **Allen L. Chickering's** account of this amazing discovery:

> "…Announcement of the finding of **the Plate** was made at a meeting of the **California Historical Society** held **April 6, 1937**, at the *Sir Francis Drake Hotel* in San Francisco, and an account of the Plate, its discovery, the speech of Dr. Bolton announcing its discovery, and the historical accounts relative to setting it up, were published by the *California Historical Society* under the title of *Drake's Plate of Brass* in 1937.

> Upon the announcement of its discovery, **Mr. William Caldeira,** a chauffeur employed by Mr. J.B. Metcalf, in Piedmont, came forward and announced that he had more than three years theretofore found the same Plate on the Laguna Ranch owned by Mr. Leland S. Murphy. This Ranch is in

Marin County and borders on Drake's Bay. At the time he found it, he had driven his then employer, **Mr. Leon Bocqueraz**, Vice Chairman of the *Bank of America National Trust and Savings Association*, to the Laguna Ranch to hunt. While Mr. Bocqueraz was engaged in hunting, Mr. Caldeira passed the time in walking around. While doing so, he saw and picked up a plate in the Y between two intersecting roads near the Laguna Ranch house at a point about **one and a half miles interior from Drake's Bay**. He states that he washed the plate in a creek and that he was able to make out the letters **"Drake"** in the signature at the foot of the plate, but could not make out any other words. He thought that the printing was foreign writing of some kind. He showed it to Mr. Bocqueraz when he returned from hunting, which Mr. Bocqueraz remembers. However, Mr. Bocqueraz was very tired and remarked that it was probably something off a ship and that he did not care to look at it. Mr. Bocqueraz stated later that he had intended to ask Caldeira to show him the plate when he got back to the Club at which he was staying, but that the matter slipped his mind. Caldeira kept it for several weeks and then, according to his story, threw it out of his automobile on the right hand side of the road from San Quentin to Kentfield in the first meadow after one leaves the intersection of the San Francisco-San Rafael road and the San Quentin-Kentfield road. It should be noted that **Caldeira** could not have thrown it far enough so that it could have fallen at the place where Shinn found it. Accordingly, some other agency than Caldeira must have intervened between the time he threw it away and the time that **Shinn** picked it up. On being shown the plate, Caldeira stated that he was sure that it was the same plate as the one he had picked up because he remembered the hole in it and because of the name "Drake" on it. He did not remember the notches at the top and bottom of the plate. He stated that at the time he found it, it was very dirty and not nearly as clear to read as when it was shown to him for identification.

Following the announcement of its discovery, **the Plate** on or about **April 12, 1937**, was physically delivered to the **University of California,** together with a sum of money for the purpose, among others, of being used for such test or **tests** as to the **genuineness** of the Plate as might seem desirable.

As was to be expected, the announcement of the discovery of the Plate was attended with great interest and some expressions of doubt as to its authenticity.

Dr. Robert G. Sproul, President of the University of California, accordingly appointed a committee, consisting of **Professors Herbert E. Bolton, J.M. Cline, Joel H. Hildebrand** and **Mr. Allen L. Chickering,**

rmine upon and have made such tests as to the authenticity of the
in its judgment seemed proper. At its first meeting the Committee
⸦ided unanimously that any tests of the Plate itself should not be made
by anyone connected with the University of California on account of the
interest of the University in the Plate. It was the Committee's belief that
the matter should be submitted only to an expert of the highest quality, not
connected with the University of California and entirely impartial. The
selection of such an individual was a matter of great difficulty and required
much correspondence, study and thought.

The public generally, especially those who were but little informed,
believed that if this or that chemist or metallurgist could have a small piece
of the metal of the Plate, he would be able to determine in a few minutes
whether it was ancient brass or not. This view was not shared by the best
informed gentlemen who were consulted, all of whom believed that it was
a question to be submitted only to an expert of the highest standing. In
spite of constant pressure and suggestions, however, the Committee decided
not to be hurried but first to make sure that it was right and then proceed.
Finally it was decided to refer the matter to **Dr. Colin G. Fink of Columbia
University, New York**, he being in the opinion of the Committee the **best
qualified** man in the **United States** to make the investigation. Dr. Fink
was indeed fortunate to be able to enlist the services of **George R.
Harrison** of **Massachusetts Institute of Technology**, a recognized **expert
in spectroscopy**. He also had the assistance and collaboration of other
eminent scientists, who are mentioned in his report which is printed herewith. The Plate itself was in the hands of **Dr. Fink** and his **associate,
Dr. Polushkin**, for more than seven months. Information submitted to
them at their request included a report on the climate and temperatures of
the region in which the Plate was found or in which it might have been set
up, by Prof. John Leighly of the University of California; a report on the
geology of these regions by **Dr. O.P. Jenkins, Chief Geologist of the
California State Mining Bureau**, and samples of soil from the place
where Shinn found the Plate, the place where Caldeira found it, and from
the site of the *Francis Drake Monument* at Point Reyes. No one taking
the trouble to read Dr. Fink's report can doubt the care, thought and industry
of which it is the result. Also it will be apparent to anyone reading his report that the determination of the factors surrounding the authenticity of
the Plate was by no means the easy matter which so many people in good
faith believed.

It is submitted that the time taken in selecting the proper expert to
make the investigation, and the time consumed in making the investigation,
have been fully justified. The results of Dr. Fink's investigation speak for
themselves.

GILOLO IN.

Tarenate   Tidore   Mutir   Machian   Bachian

Quam mirificè a Rege Moluccarum tubarū clangorem
admirante, introvectus fuerit, delineatio.

*Sir Francis Drake's welcome by the King of the Moluccas.
Vignette from the Judocus Hondius map, circa 1595.*

DRAKE'S PLATE OF BRASS
AUTHENTICATED

The Report on the Plate of Brass
by Colin G. Fink & E. P. Polushkin

Frontispiece of The Report on the Plate of Brass.

CHAPTER III

The Report on the Plate of Brass
by Colin G. Fink and E.P. Polushkin

Professor H.E. Bolton, of the **University of California,** submitted to the senior author for examination a metal plate with an engraved inscription, attributed to Sir Francis Drake. The complete text of the inscription is given in the pamphlet, *Drake's Plate of Brass - Evidence of His visit to California in 1579,* San Francisco, California Historical Society, MCMXXXVII. Professor Bolton advised that this plate had been found on the northern shore of San Francisco Bay in 1936, that the text of the inscription on the plate corresponds closely with the data cited in the book, *The World Encompassed by Sir Francis Drake,* published in London in 1628 and based on the notes of Chaplain Francis Fletcher, one of Drake's party, and that, in all probability, the plate submitted to us for authentication is the one that had been fastened to a post by Drake's order during his stay at California in 1579. We were requested to make a careful study of the plate in order to ascertain whether it was genuine.

Although the text of the inscription closely corresponds with Fletcher's data, it was not considered a sufficient proof of the genuineness of the plate, since anybody could have referred to *The World Encompassed by Sir Francis Drake,* composed an inscription based on data recorded therein, and then engraved it on a brass plate. Objects of art, as well as historical relics, are so often copies, or so basely fraudulent that such a critical attitude was fully justifiable. Accordingly, it was decided to undertake an independent, thorough examination of the plate from every possible angle, with the object of uncovering any and all proofs of fact or fraud.

It was necessary to examine under the microscope not only the metal structure but also all details on the surface of the plate, its workmanship and patina. In addition, the metal, patina and soils in which the plate had lain buried **had to be analyzed,** aside from many other tests detailed below. The results of certain of these tests had to be compared with data on modern brass as well as with data on well-known old brass of **the period** to which the **Drake Plate** would belong. The large number of tests involved in this study and the difficulty and delay experienced in obtaining acceptable specimens for comparison study were chiefly responsible for the prolonged period of this investigation.

The following thorough investigations were undertaken:

(1) The Shape and Dimensions of the Plate
...The crude workmanship is especially evident in the

apearance of the hole which, according to Fletcher, was made to hold the sixpence. This hole was very roughly cut by means of a chisel...

...If the plate is genuine, it was not rolled, since the process of rolling brass had not yet been introduced at the time of Drake. The shaping of large brass plates during that period was done with heavy hammers...It appears certain, however, that the plate was cut from a larger plate and with a chisel, since the cut edge still bears chisel marks...

In order to verify the above assumptions that a hole of a given dimension could hold a sixpence coin, we placed a sixpence of Elizabeth's time in the hole. We found that the groove and prongs held the coin well in place...The rose behind the Queen's head is seen in the photograph...

A Queen Elizabeth I sixpence Inserted into Hole of the Plate of Brass. Natural Size.

(2) Examination of the Engraved Letters

...The importance of this individual examination is self-evident because in case of fraud there is always a chance of finding a hidden area which would disclose a fresh, corrosion-free surface of the metal or a trace of artificial treatment...*No indication or clue of artificial patination of any kind was discovered by us in the grooves...*

...An interesting detail which we observed in the lettering was the parallel lines, a series of fine, parallel grooves located near many of the letters...The closeness of these lines to each other and their parallelism indicate that they could not have been made by hand one by one. If they had been made with a hand chisel (which is most probable), a special holder for the chisel fastened to a bench might have been used...upon consulting **Mr. S.V. Grancsay**, an expert on armor at the **Metropolitan Museum of Art, New York City**, he stated that *parallel lines such as we observed in the plate were occasionally found on old brass armor*. It is also possible that, due to limited equipment of the machine shop on board Drake's ship, some unusual, home-made, mechanical device was used in cutting the letters into the plate. The chisel may have been securely fixed over the plate and the plate moved about after each groove had been cut...

...As in any old brass, the surface of the plate shows numerous defects such as cracks, pits and corroded areas...

Lettering on "Plate of Brass" - Parallel Lines as such Found on Old Brass Armor.

(3) Indentations

The face or front surface of the plate has many indentations, large and small, scattered all over the plate. Examination showed that these are not accidental markings but were made by a tool or weapon: they all show more or less similar deformation lines on the depressed surface...It is possible that the indentations on the plate were made by the Indians who were afraid of a mysterious or hostile power of the plate and after the departure of Drake, tried to destroy the plate by striking its surface with their tomahawks; they were not familiar with the toughness of metals.

This assumption of ours was fully supported by **Dr. W.C. Orchard**, of the **Museum of the American Indian, New York City,** whom we consulted in regard to these indentations. He expressed the opinion that indentations of this kind were, most probably, made by stone axes or celts used by the Indians. A typical view of an Indian ax is shown in the photograph. When the surface of a modern brass sheet was struck with this ax in oblique direction, the indentations produced were very similar to those on the plate...Small, triple indentations visible in the center and on the right side may have been made by a stone ax with a blunted edge.

Indian Stone Ax used to Duplicate the Indentations.
Natural Size.

(4) Examination of the Back Surface of the Plate

...All of the results of the examination of the coating on the plate point to the conclusion that the coating is a *genuine patina gradually formed during a long period of time...*

(5) Examination of the Material from the Coin Groove

...The observed results of heating the bulk of the black material taken from the coin groove were, in general, the same as those upon heating the scrapings from the coating of the plate; that is, the black substance of the powder from the coin groove was largely changed into pale orange, red and brown particles with only occasional inclusions of black mineral.

Dimensions of Hole cut in "Plate of Brass" to hold Sixpence.
Natural Size.

(6) Microstructure of the Metal and Patina of the Plate

...*Inclusions:* Under the microscope the metal revealed an excessive amount of inclusions...The large amount of impurities present is very characteristic of all old metals due to the comparatively crude methods employed in their smelting and refining. In the 16th Century or earlier, all brass was made by smelting copper and zinc ore (calamine), together with fine charcoal. Salt was added as a flux... The chemical identification of the inclusions in an old metal is even more important than their quantity in determining the genuineness of such old metal...we feel justified in stating that such inclusions do not occur in modern brass...

In regard to the number and nature of inclusions, the metal of the Plate showed a close similarity to that of well-known old brass which was examined by us for comparison's sake...Numerous inclusions appear in the photomicrograph of this old brass as black dots; they are scattered throughout the metal and are mostly of a dark brown color, although some are distinctly red...In old brass, the cracks are often caused by the presence of impurities and in this case the peculiar, wavy arrangement of the fine inclusions was very indicative. If the metal had been rolled, the inclusions would be strung out in virtually straight lines parallel to the direction of rolling. The rolling process began to be used in the copper and brass industry at the end of the 17th Century; before that time, all brass objects had been worked by hammer. The use of large hammers might have the same effect on the structure as rolls, but small hammers necessarily produce local irregularities in the structure and particularly in the arrangement of the inclusions...

...We could not find even a slight indication that the plate before us had been rolled. On the other hand, *we did find evidence that the plate had been hammered.* The character of the surface of the plate, as well as the wavy arrangement of the inclusions, point to hammering rather than to rolling as the method used in making the plate...

Cracks: Cracks are very common in old brass. In this specimen we found them in every section examined.

Corrosion of the Metal: The original, exposed edge of the cross section of the polished specimen of the metal of the plate was found to be corroded...

...Accumulation of metallic copper as a result of corrosion is very frequently found in corroded specimens of brass and bronze.

All of the results of our microscopic study of the cross section of the patina of the plate confirm our conclusion arrived at after the preliminary examination of the patina, gradually formed during a long period of time.

(7) Structural Constituents of the Metal

…It is well known that alpha brass in cast condition consists of two different portions of alpha solution, copper-rich and zinc-rich, which have different colors under the microscope. In modern brass this difference in the chemical composition of two portions of alpha is entirely eliminated by subsequent mechanical and thermal treatment, but in old brass, which was worked by crude methods, a trace of the original heterogeneity can always be expected.

(8) Chemical Composition of the Metal

…About one-third of the specimen used for microscopic examination…was cut off and sent to **Professor George R. Harrison** of the **Massachusetts Institute of Technology** with the request that he make a preliminary qualitative determination of elements present in the metal. The following results were reported by him:

Major constituents: copper and zinc.
Minor constituents: magnesium, iron and cadmium.
Small amount: silver, silicon and tin.
Very small amount: calcium, aluminum, manganese and antimony.

The proportion of the two principal elements, copper and zinc, has already been determined approximately by the microscopic examination which showed that the metal is brass with 34-39 per cent zinc. A more accurate determination of the zinc percentage was of no importance. Of the three minor elements, magnesium was the most interesting since it is not as common in modern brass as are iron and cadmium. If it is present in larger amounts than found in modern brass, this will suggest an old origin of the plate because all brass of Drake's time was produced from mixtures of copper and calamine, and the latter mineral always contains magnesium...

A quantitative estimate of the silver present was also of interest because copper used in the making of brass in Drake's time was not refined and, in case the copper contained silver, the latter should have passed into the brass.

For these reasons it was necessary to analyze the specimen quantitatively for magnesium and silver, and Professor Harrison reported the following proportion of these elements:

Magnesium: 102 parts per million or 0.0102%
Silver: 3.6 parts per million or 0.00036%

...We were not able to find in the literature any indication of the presence of magnesium in modern brass amounting to more than 0.002 per cent...Since as much as 0.01% magnesium was found in the brass of the plate, this would indicate that the brass is very likely not modern...

the amount of magnesium found...does suggest ancient origin...

...According to information received from Professor Bolton, the plate might have wandered from one place to another. At our request, **Mr. Allen L. Chickering** sent us four samples of soil collected: (1) at the place where Mr. Shinn found the plate: (2) just above the beach at Drake's Bay, below the monument erected in 1916 by the Sir Francis Drake Association; (3) at the base of the monument, in the premises of the Coast Guard Station on the Drake's Bay side of Pt. Reyes; and (4) at the place where Caldeira found the plate.

These samples were analyzed in Professor Harrison's laboratory...

Thus, spectrographic analysis of the soil substantiated our assumption that the patina had been formed on the plate as a natural product of chemical changes in the metal caused by atmospheric conditions and by contact of the plate with the minerals of the surrounding soil.

Summary

(1) There is no doubt whatsoever that the dark coating on the surface of the plate is a **natural patina** formed slowly over a period of many years.

(2) Numerous surface defects and **imperfections** usually associated with **old brass** were found on the plate.

(3) Particles of **mineralized plant tissue** are firmly imbedded in the surface of the plate. This is likewise a very positive proof of the **age of the plate**.

(4) Cross sections of the brass plate show (a) an **excessive amount of impurities;** and (b) **chemical inhomogeneity**; as well as (c) **variation in grain size.** All three of these characteristics indicate **a brass of old origin**.

(5) Among the impurities found in the brass of the plate there is **magnesium,** which is present far in **excess of** the amount occurring in **modern brass**.

(6) There are numerous indications that the plate was **not made by rolling** but was **made by hammering**, as was the common practice in **Drake's time**.

Conclusion

On the basis of the above **six distinct finds**, as well as other data herewith recorded, it is our opinion that the brass plate examined by us is the **genuine Drake Plate** referred to in the book, *The World Encompassed by Sir Francis Drake*, published in 1628.

The report herewith appended on the examination of the Drake Plate is respectfully submitted
to the owners of the Plate by:

Colin G. Fink,
Ph. D., D. Sc.

E. P. Polushkin

Electrochemical Laboratories,
Columbia University,
New York City.
Sept. 16, 1938.

Report Submitted by Colin G. Fink, Ph.D., D.Sc. and E.P. Polushkin,
Electrochemical Laboratories, Columbia University.

Fleet Admiral Chester W. Nimitz, U.S.N., points toward the cove where Drake set up his encampment and careened the Golden Hinde in 1579. It should be noted that the tiny model of the Golden Hinde is greatly over scale in comparison with the map on which it rests.

CHAPTER IV

"Francis Drake Luncheon Address"
by Fleet Admiral Chester W. Nimitz, U.S.N.
and "Drake Plate" Presentation

On November 15, 1962, *Honorary Chairman of the Drake Navigators Guild, Admiral Chester W. Nimitz, USN* gave the following Drake Luncheon Address:

We are here to honor **Francis Drake,** the first English voyager who made contact on the coast of California and laid claim for his Queen to land in what is now continental United States. This was an event often overlooked in honoring Drake as the first commander to circumnavigate the globe. Yet its importance takes precedence today as the first actual link between England and the United States.

Drake's voyage in 1577 to 1580 called for individual resourcefulness far and beyond today's requirements of orbiting space. The intervening centuries have brought such great advances in all fields of knowledge allied with navigation, that it is difficult for the layman today to assess the basic difficulties that confronted 16th century seamen.

In honoring Drake we also acknowledge our debt to the early navigators, philosophers, and mathematicians for their contributions to man's knowledge in relation to global navigation. Although this list is too long to be given here, mention must be made of Prince Henry the Navigator (1394-1460). Under his inspiration the art of navigation was developed out of the art of pilotage to meet the needs of oceanic explorers and seamen. These needs were to find their position when out of sight of land, to ascertain the location of new lands when first discovered, and to be able to return to them…

…That *Drake also claimed land on the Pacific Coast of America* may have been incidental. It was, however, the finding of a proper "portus" in which to secure water, refit the *Golden Hinde*, refresh his men and revictual the ship on the coast of California, which made the successful continuance of the voyage possible.

Francis Drake's arrival on the California coast was by sea. His departure from England and his return to Plymouth were by sea. His entire operation was a navigational feat in the face of all the limitations of knowledge, lack of accurate charts and instruments, and the hardships that beset any extended voyage in a small ship of the 16th century. So it was logical for the *Drake Navigators Guild* to take these known constants as their primary basis of research. The navigational approach enabled the Guild to coordinate the facts and put the pieces together to pinpoint Drake's California site.

In following this course, the Guild is alert to the accomplishments of all who have contributed to the serious study of Drake in California. The organizations sponsoring this meeting have made distinct contributions, primarily through individuals, some of whom no longer grace the earth. Among these, I would first like to pay tribute to Dr. George Davidson.

Dr. Davidson's monograph, *The Identification of Francis Drake's Anchorage in 1579,* published in 1890 by the *California Historical Society*, is outstanding among America's contributions to research on Drake. It presents the mature, carefully considered judgment of a man who served the United States Coast and Geodetic Survey with distinction for fifty years. In the 1850's he was in charge of charting our West coast for the first definitive Survey. He was a versatile scientist and a prolific writer in the fields of geography, geodesy and history. Dr. Davidson's library, a highly valued source of coastal studies, is now at the *California Academy of Sciences*, of which he was president for sixteen years prior to his death in 1911.

To **Allen L. Chickering,** past president of the *California Historical Society*, we also pay tribute. He was to a major degree responsible for the original securing and authentication of the famed **Drake "Plate of Brass,"** now on permanent display at the *Bancroft Library in the University of California.*

The *Sir Francis Drake Association*, whose specific interest is the first reading of a Christian service in English from the Book of Common Prayer within the boundaries of continental United States, has also kept the Drake tradition alive in California.

The heritage bond of our common tongue is exemplified by the *English Speaking Union* in its sponsorship, together with others, of today's Drake Luncheon.

Professors at the University of California have made major contributions. To name a few, I mention **Dr. Robert F. Heizer** for his study of *Francis Drake and the California Indians in 1579,* the eminent historians **Dr. Herbert E. Bolton** and **Henry R. Wagner**.

You have heard men's names, but there are women who have been completely entranced and captured by the Drake saga. Some of the finest work in research on Drake, in England, has been produced by such women as **Zelia Nuttal; E.G.R. Taylor**, and **Irene A. Wright** – to name of few.

The Drake Navigators Guild, in their thorough scholarly research on Drake in California, have made a most important contribution. The Guild's findings are respected by their British confreres, notably, **R.A. Skelton,** Curator of the Library

*Dr. Rockwell D. Hunt, President Emeritus of the Conference of California Historical Societies, and H.R.H. Prince Philip, The Duke of Edinburgh, compare notes on Sir Francis Drake's **Nova Albion, the first New England,** prior to the Drake Luncheon at which Dr. Hunt was honored.*

and Maps at the ***British Museum;*** **A.A. Cumming, F.M.A.,** Curator of Buckland Abbey, formerly the home of Sir Francis Drake and now ***England's Drake Museum***, and Curator of the ***City Museum and Art Gallery*** at Plymouth.

The Friends of Buckland Abbey through their president, **Lord Mount Edgecumbe**, are fully conversant with Guild research, which is being carried on with interested cooperation from **F.G.G. Carr**, Curator of the ***National Maritime Museum***, at Greenwich, where **Lieutenant Commander D.W. Waters**, Curator of ***Navigation and Astronomy***, also gives freely of his time and attention.

H.R.H. Prince Philip, The Duke of Edinburgh, as Patron of ***The Friends of Buckland Abbey*** and as a trustee of the ***National Maritime Museum***, has followed the work of the Guild with interest. So also has the eminent historian **A.L. Rowse,** ***Fellow of All Soul's College, Oxford***, whose brilliant writing on 16th century England has won him international acclaim. Dr. Rowse is currently doing research on Shakespeare at the ***Huntington Library*** in Southern California. On visiting the Drake site at ***Drake's Cove*** recently, he remarked that the Cove was the sort of

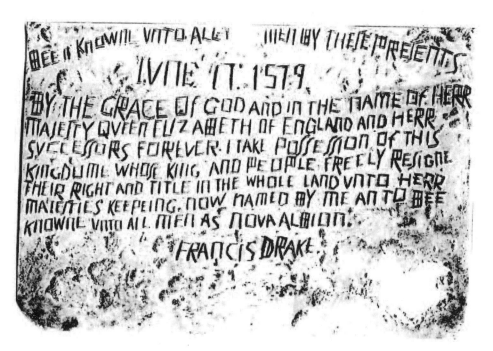

Francis Drake's "Plate of Brass," June 17, 1579.

"portus" most sought by 16th century mariners for the purpose of reconditioning their ships.

The **British Admiralty Hydrographic Office** has made a major contribution to further Guild research. The United States Coast and Geodetic Survey and our own Hydrographic Office, which operates within the **United States Navy Department**, have contributed important data and continue to aid us immeasurably. Navigational and cartographical assistance has also been afforded the **Drake Navigators Guild** by France, Holland and other maritime countries of Europe...

The sea produced the first and only universal language understood throughout the world. The **International Code** for ships at sea – starting with flags, drums and cannon – has for generations been a means of **world-wide communication**. It stands as the first break-through of language barriers.

A like need applies today when world cooperation must be on a navigational basis for future explorations in space. This is the type of cooperation all countries find desirable to cultivate. Men of the sea are less inclined to division, and more prone to pool their findings. These are ideal conditions for man's progress...

PRESENTATION

Among our historians, I have purposefully delayed mentioning one name. He is here as an honored guest.

This scholar does not admit to being the first to recognize the land in California claimed by Drake for Queen Elizabeth as **America's "First New England."** In fact, he states in a recent letter to the president of the **Drake Navigators Guild**: "A good many years ago Judge John F. Davis of San Francisco called attention to an '**earlier New England**' in North America, referring to '**Nova Albion**' claimed by Drake. **Mr. Charles E. Chapman** of the **University of California** and other historians have eulogized Drake, as you know, and have emphasized 'the importance of his work affecting the future of California.'" He goes on to say, "I do not know how many writers may have used the name 'New England.' It may be that I made a more explicit point of it than other writers."

On this point he was more than explicit. He widely disseminated the term **"First New England."** In the 1911 school history textbook by this fine historian, he clearly presented the facts about **"New Albion"** – Albion being a name selected by **Francis Drake** because his own country "was sometime so called." Later, in his fine volume, **California Firsts**, he specifically identified New Albion as our **"First New England."**

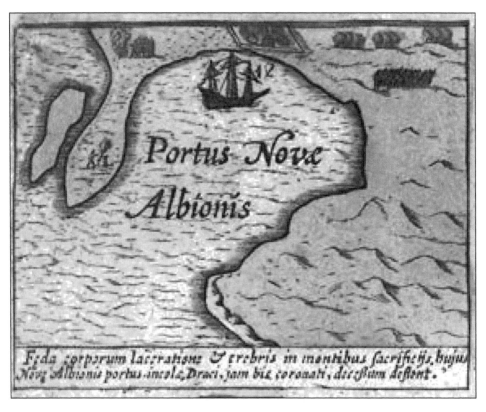

Vignette from the Judocus Hondius Map, showing the
Portus Nove Albionis where Drake anchored.

…I am speaking of the **President Emeritus of the Conference of California Historical Societies,** who is often referred to as "dean of California historians." I have a presentation to make to **Dr. Rockwell D. Hunt.**

Drake "Plate of Brass" Facsimile Reproduction Presentation

It gives me great pleasure, Dr. Hunt, to offer you this facsimile reproduction of the **Drake "Plate of Brass."** It has been *framed in driftwood from Drake's Bay* for you as a token of acknowledgment and esteem, with the compliments of the Drake Navigators Guild.[1]

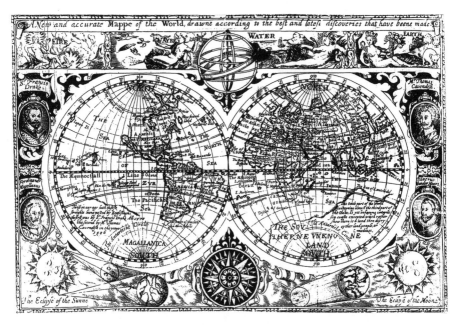

*A New and Accurate Mappe of the World, drawne according to the Best
and Latest Discoveries that have been Made. From, The World
Encompassed by Sir Francis Drake, 1628.*

CHAPTER V

History Rewritten – 1977
by The Bancroft Library, University of California, Berkeley

The first six pages of *The Plate of Brass Re-examined – A Report Issued by The Bancroft Library, University of California, Berkeley - 1977,* cites twenty-two quotations from the California Historical Society's 1938 publication, **The Plate of Brass: Evidence of the Visit of Francis Drake to California in the Year 1579,** adding that,

> "The Report of Fink and Polushkin submitted on September 16, 1938 also **touched lightly** on **the engraved letters,** and members of President Sproul's committee ventured some opinion on the lettering and the language, but apparently there was general recognition that until the antiquity of the brass was established, there was no point in investigating what was incised upon it. So essentially the **so-called authentication of the Plate of Brass** in 1938 **was determined** by **metallurgical examination…**nevertheless, the contention that the Plate was the work of a modern forger continued to be expressed…**Professor Caley** (Earle R. Caley of the Frick Chemical Laboratory, **Princeton University**) was skeptical about the Plate for several diverse reasons.

First of all, he pointed to published analyses of English brasses of the 15th and 16th Centuries that showed their **zinc content to be under 30%,** a finding comparable to published analyses of 19 German brasses of those dates, only **two of which** were **within the range of 34 to 39%** found in **the Plate** by Fink and Polushkin…Professor Caley observed too that 'the alleged mineralized plant tissue in the coin groove' might well be nothing more than 'wood ash imbedded in the surface' since this 'would have a like structure under the microscope.' He also expressed uneasiness about a different, but equally equivocal aspect of the coin groove which he judged to be 'less corroded than the metal on the back of the plate,' although one would expect equal corrosion everywhere…' Professor Caley indicated that he was countering what he liked least about the Fink and Polushkin Report: 'the ignoring of alternative explanations and contrary evidence…'

Dr. Harlow, (Vincent T. Harlow, Keeper, Rhodes House Library, **Oxford University**) in a letter of July 22, 1937…thought, 'it is inconceivable that **Drake could not have produced a more imposing piece of brass** — he had an orchestra on board as well as brass guns and fittings and a cargo of

Spanish plunder, and secondly, that he could not find among his ship's company someone capable of **producing a better effort than this clumsy botch.** Apart from the possible executants, there was **the Chaplain**—an artist, some of whose drawings have survived.'

Beyond the crude physical appearance of the Plate, Dr. Harlow was put off by the text itself. He declared, 'Drake would have instructed **his engraver** in an important matter like this to put **ELIZABETH** in the centre & at the head of the plate. He had his own commission to consult for guidance & in any case there were many gentlemen on board the *Golden Hind*...who would know the familiar form of words by heart...The phrases on the plate – **'I take possession of,'** and **'in the whole land'** as well as the structure of the sentence strike me as 20th century instead of 16th century...' Captain R.B. Haselden was equally disturbed by what he called 'the curious M's and N's.'

Professor Bolton found that Haselden's 'testimony is purely negative and is incomplete, for no one, presumably, has seen all the N's and M's made in the 16th century. Moreover, it is quite conceivable that a person working with crude equipment might easily depart from all conventional forms.' **Professor Bolton** went on to declare that '**the objection** that the **position** of **the Queen's name is not 'normal'** is only **personal opinion**, and **not evidence**. Moreover, the circumstances under which Drake erected his tablet were anything but normal, and normal results would hardly be expected.' To another objection put forward by Haselden, Professor Bolton declared, 'I see **no evidence** that the first line ('**Bee it knowne unto all men, etc.**') was an '**afterthought.'** Why not first make the slots for the nails, then adjust the inscription to them? It could be done this way just as well. But if it was an afterthought all the better. **A first-rate faker** would presumably have **more time than Drake's man** had, and would be less likely to need to add an afterthought...'

...Several other kinds of study were projected. These included not only **physical and chemical tests**, but scrutiny directed at historical aspects of the Plate. The latter investigations were addressed entirely to matters of **text and orthography**...

The first several questions related to the **lettering on the Plate** was raised most forcefully by **an alumna** of the Berkeley campus in the **Class of 1921, Ethel Ames Sagen**, who contended that there was an 'alphabetalogical fact that the letter J did not enter the English alphabet until after Drake's death.' A little investigation of this interesting point suggested that, like everything else in this world, the issue was a bit more complicated than it appeared to be at first. The noted bibliographer, **R.B. McKerrow** cast light on this subject when he declared: '**It is well known that until the 16th century, i and j were, as a general rule, regarded merely as two forms of the same letter,**'...but 'there was an upper-case letter approximating in shape in Gothic founts rather to the modern J than I, but serving indifferently for either'...

Professor Wayne Shumaker of the **Department of English at Berkeley,** in considering this matter, wondered whether the J might not have come into England 'in handwriting and been accepted only tardily by printers? In general, the usage of printers is conservative.' **The letters** that Mrs. Sagen **questioned** were the '**I's**' in **IVNE** (line two), **MAIESTY** (line four) and **MAIESTIES** (line eight)...

Attention was also given to the other lettering, particularly the **B, P, R, M, N**...Although **Professor Shumaker** pointed out that this subject is not in his area of professional competence, he nevertheless wondered, 'why should a forger have invented unknown letter-forms, knowing that anything odd might awaken suspicion?...As for the letters, who can know the source of their odd forms? People still sometimes invent their own letter-forms. The first of the odd letters, B, may have suggested to the inscriber the opportunity for making a pious cross by the addition of an extra vertical, and the scheme then carried out also in the P's and R's. The M's and N's may have been simplified from cursive letters in order to facilitate the chiseling process (as anybody who has carved his name in wood would understand). The extra vertical in one M was probably sheer error. The long S's would have been just that in a cursive script; if the metal smith was told to 'make all the letters capitals,' his limited literacy may have co-operated with his desire to avoid curves to produce the forms we have.' Another **Professor** of the **Department of English at Berkeley, Alan Nelson,** offered the guess that the added vertical in B, P, and R might have been a kind of attempt at the effect of publication by a **zealous**, but rather **unlettered workman**...

The subject was referred to **Giles E. Dawson** and **Laetitia Yeandle**, the authors of ***Elizabethan Handwriting, 1500-1600*** (1966). Mrs. Yeandle: "The spelling is surprisingly modern, and the chief anachronistic one, '**Herr**' a very unlikely variant that is not recorded in the OED." (The spelling 'Herr' had been challenged previously, but an example dated about **1580** had been discovered in a **manuscript** cited by **Mr. Allen Chickering** in the **California Historical Society Quarterly,** Volume 18, Number 3, September 1939, pages 251-252). Mr. Chickering states:*

---

*Author's inclusion of Mr. Chickering's cited article, in text.

"In an article entitled *'Some Notes with Regard to Drake's Plate of Brass,'* in the September, 1937, number of this Quarterly, I discussed a manuscript which antedated the Plate by more than a hundred years and which contained instances of spelling like that in the Plate. There were two words on the Plate, however – 'keepeing' and 'herr' which at that time I had not succeeded in finding elsewhere with exactly the same spelling. Since then I have come across the word 'keepe' in *The Famous Voyage of Sir Francis Drake into the South Sea, and there hence about the whole globe of the Earth, begun in the yeere of our Lord, 1577* and an Elizabethan manuscript, *State Papers Domestic, Elizabeth 144, No. 51,* in which it appears several times; And the form 'kepeing' occurs many times in the earlier manuscript previously discussed. It seems, therefore, quite logical that 'keepeing' might also have been used in manuscripts of the period. To some, the spelling *herr* seemed a reason for doubting the authenticity of the Plate. Captain R.B. Haselden, for instance, in his article, *'Is the Drake Plate of Brass Genuine?'* referred to it as **'the bizarre spelling of *herr*.'** On the other hand, this spelling seems to others to point to the authenticity of the Plate. J.A. Williamson, for example, in the *Geographical Journal* for June, 1938, wrote as follows:

'The question of genuineness at present turns on the evidence provided by the Plate itself. Various details in the inscription have been challenged, but in the present writer's opinion the only serious difficulty is in the spelling **HERR,** occurring three times. He cannot recall ever meeting with the spelling in an Elizabethan document, although the word is so common that he must have seen it many times in the writings of the period. At first sight this word **HERR** appeared to condemn the inscription as spurious, but on reflection it seemed to point with equal force in the contrary direction. If the forger was sufficiently competent to evolve an inscription which in all other respects of spelling and phrasing is unexceptionable, why should he make a blunder so elementary? On the whole it seems just as likely that the word **HERR** was so spelled by an Elizabethan as by a pseudo-Elizabethan. Ventilation of this point may well have the result of producing some authenticated example of *herr.*'

As a result of my study on this subject, I am firmly convinced that reference should be made to *manuscripts,* and not to printed matter, to test the spelling in what is, in effect, also a *manuscript.* It may be, and probably was, true, that proof-reading in 1579 was not the exact science which it is today, but there probably was *some* attempt at standardization of spelling in printed books. In manuscripts it was different. As I stated in the September, 1937 *Quarterly*: 'As a result of my study (of a ***manuscript*** prepared over one hundred years earlier) I am firmly of the belief that no attention whatever was paid to spelling so long as the pronunciation of the result was substantially like that to which the writer was accustomed.'

Further investigation has only tended to confirm this opinion. Elizabethan manuscripts are not very plentiful in the vicinity, but a few months ago I happened to run across a quotation in ***Francis Drake & Other Early Explorers Along the Pacific Coast***, by Dr. John W. Robertson, in which the project of a corporation to settle the lands discovered by Drake was discussed and in which the word ***herr*** appeared…The *manuscript* of the project for such a colonization corporation was to be found as ***No. 44 in Volume 144, State Papers, Domestic, Elizabeth***. I thereupon sent to the ***Royal Geographical Society,*** London, and through the great kindness of the Librarian, Mr. G.R. Crone, I obtained a Photostat of the entire prospectus, which is believed to be in the handwriting of *Sir Francis Waysyngham*, of **Queen Elizabeth's court**, and to have been prepared in **1580.** The *manuscript* is reproduced herewith (excerpted):

A PRO<u>I</u>ECT OF A CORPORATYON OF SOCHE AS SHALL VENTEUR <u>V</u>NTO SOCHE DOMYNIONS AND CONTREYS SYTUATE BAYONDE THE EQUYNOCTYALL LINE

Imprimis y(t) y(t) may please **herr** Ma(tie) to graunt lyke p'vyleges as have bene graunted by **herr** H (s)…sub<u>i</u>ectes tradying into the dominions of the Emperor of Russia.
Item that in consyderatyon of the late notable dyscoverye made by Francys Drake of sooche dominions as are scytuated beyonde the said Equynoctyall lyne…."

(The above reproduction of the original 1580 manuscript fully validates the authenticity of the **Elizabethan spelling** of "<u>i</u>" in lieu of "j" and **"<u>herr</u>"** in lieu of "her," removing the negative arguments put forth by Mrs. Ethel Ames Sagen; Mrs. Laetitia Yeandle and Captian R.B. Haselden.)*

---

*Author's words in parentheses.

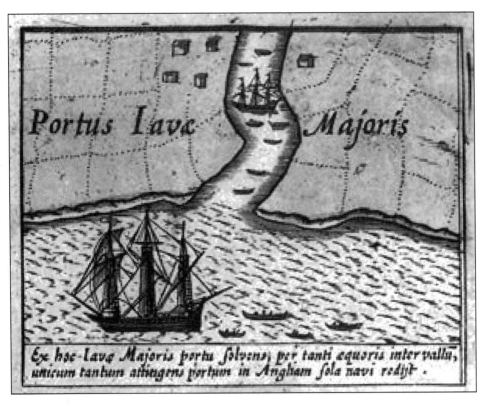

Vignette from the circa 1595 Hondius map showing "Portus Iave (Java) Majoris.

The text of the plate also disturbed **Professor Barnes** (Thomas G. Barnes of the **Department of History at Berkeley**). He could not think of any instance in which a common person (**Sir Francis Drake**) performs an act and declares that he does it "by the grace of God." Furthermore, Professor Barnes thought the terminology in reference to Queen Elizabeth quite improper and suggested that it should be something like, "Elizabeth, by the grace of God, Queen of England, Ireland and France (and possibly 'etc'.), defender of the faith." (This author has consulted charters and proclamations issued by British Monarchs, to include *The First Virginia Charter* dated April 10, 1606, which customarily commence thus, "James, by the grace of God, King of England, Scotland, France and Ireland, Defender of the Faith, etc..." However, these monarchs are **personally** making and signing decrees, whereas *Francis Drake makes a claim on behalf of* Elizabeth, his sovereign. It is not King James – nor Elizabeth I – speaking, but a subject of the Queen, taking possession of the territory *on her behalf –* necessitating different wording).*

This matter also engaged the concern of **Mrs. Yeandle** who wrote: "I also find the wording of the inscription uncharacteristic of official and semi-official documents. The opening phrase is only halfway convincing. One often comes across 'Know all men by these presents that I, A.B. do...' Why was **Drake's name** (and **descriptive title**) not incorporated here as well as at the end in the witness clause? I think the queen has not been given due consideration, despite the added number of strokes this would have entailed. She usually is styled 'our sovereign lady Elizabeth by the grace of God queen of England, France and Ireland (or, of England, France and Ireland queen) defender of the faith, etc.' The date too is in a curious position. It might have been included in the first part of the document but in a document addressed to the world at large as this is, it would more probably have been placed at the end, 'given at ___ this 17th (or more likely XVIIth day of June 1579 (or, in the one and twentieth or XXIst year of the reign of our sovereign lady Elizabeth...)

...A letter was sent to the outstanding authority on the history of metallurgy, **Dr. Cyril Stanley Smith, Professor Emeritus of the Massachusetts Institute of Technology**...His inclination was to accept the **Fink-Polushkin Report** as "in the main plausible," though he had several quibbles with it. The first of these was "the **authenticity** of supposed **16th century brass** on the basis of **high zinc content**." But he pointed out too, that "on the critical question of the zinc content, it should be noted that (**Fink-Polushkin**) do not base **their 34-39 per cent figure** on analyses but

---

*Author's words in parentheses.

deduce from the presence of a few small particles of the beta phase." Dr. Smith also pointed out that a high zinc content could be found in some early non-English and non-European brass for "samples of **brass with 34-40% zinc** dating from the **16th and 17th century** have been **found in India and Java**, though I suppose trans-pacific migration of the plate is rather unlikely..."

(Refuting **Professor Earle R. Caley**, of the Frick Chemical Laboratory, Princeton University's negative argument concerning the 34-39% zinc content of Drake's Plate of Brass, is **Dr. Cyril Stanley Smith**, of the Massachusetts Institute of Technology's affirmation that "samples of brass with 34-40% zinc dating from the 16th and 17th century have been found in India and Java." The famed *1595 Hondius Map* indicating present-day Drake's Bay as *Portus Nove Albionis*, also pinpoints *Portus Javae Majoris* where Francis Drake anchored his ships while circumnavigating the world – from whence 16th century brass, used for the Plate of Brass could have originated; *Portus Javae Majoris* being frequented by other ships enroute as well).*

Dr. Smith emphasized "that scientific study...of factors that can be measured with some certainty by themselves provide indecisive historical evidence," for, "**I firmly believe** that **evidence** from the viewpoint of a **materials scientist** is **not** in itself **sufficient** to form a historical conclusion."

...**Since the point of a hoax** is to show up the person **who is gulled** and since no one ever came along to reveal a fraud, **defenders of the Plate** contended that such a lack of revelation was in itself an argument against the idea of a hoax...Other skeptics have put forward still another reason why, if there was a hoax, it was not revealed by the perpetrator...

Such guesses about a hoax and the ostensible reasons for failure to reveal it are intriguing, as are all questions concerned with the Plate. It remains a fascinating object. Over forty years after its finding the **Plate of Brass** still tantalizes all who take an interest in it. Such interest has led to the present report, undertaken without prejudice toward or against authenticity. Obviously the evidence it assembles has turned out to be essentially negative. Nevertheless, the report is not issued in a partisan spirit. It is presented instead to provide the best information now available about the Plate, made with the recognition that this will probably not be accepted everywhere as the definitive or conclusive word on the subject. In this enquiry the Plate itself has been carefully safeguarded against damage so as

*Author's words in parentheses.

to remain unmutilated for other persons to study as new techniques and new ideas emerge. Here, then, are **the findings completed in 1977** for issuance by **The Bancroft Library.** Doubtless at later dates other inquiries and further commentary will be forthcoming from different sources to probe again into the nature and origin of an artifact that has attracted so much attention since its discovery.

James D. Hart
Director
The Bancroft Library
July 1977"

An additional pamphlet by **James D. Hart, Director of The Bancroft Library, University of California, Berkeley (revised May, 2001)** states that, "an X-ray diffraction investigation by the **Department of Materials Science and Mineral Engineering of the University of California, Berkeley** led to the decision that the 'plate was produced by modern rolling process rather than having been made by hammer shaping,' the only means known in Drake's time for creating such a large piece of flat brass…"

(However, refuting **James D. Hart's** above-cited statement, is the report of the world's leading experts in *Drake's Plate of Brass Authenticated – The Report on the Plate of Brass* (California Historical Society), who, after thorough investigation and examination, concluded that the "**plate of brass**" was irrefutably **hammered, and not rolled.**)*

*Author's words in parentheses.

Meigg's Wharf, and View of San Francisco, circa early 1850's.
Courtesy of California State Library.

CHAPTER VI

California's "Gold Rush" – or "God Rush?"

The early social aspects in California presented phases of life found nowhere else on the American Continent. Primarily, people came to make money. It was this that filled with passengers every vessel of every class that left for this State from the ports of the East by the way of Cape Horn, and that poured legions of people across the Isthmus of Panama from **1849-1860.** It was the love of gold which sent the more than thousands of trains over the plains, across the Rocky Mountains, through the alkaline waste of the Great American Desert, and over the giddy heights of the Sierra Nevada Mountains, to this new El Dorado.[1]

No man has attempted to summarize and give to the world the sufferings, by sea and land, of the vast numbers of men who reached the mines on the American River in **1847-51.** Nor has the least glimpse been given of the numberless graves in the ocean, across the Isthmus and on the plains, of those who died in their struggles to reach a land that was to give to all, **"Gold! Gold!!**

So easy to get and so hard to hold," until want, with its deceptive fingers, should haunt them no more. Not since the days of Peter the Hermit rallying Christendom to rescue the tomb of the Saviour of our fallen race, had there been seen such a gathering of the nations; and perhaps, not again in a thousand years will the world again set its face to another California. On the American River, **from 1847-1856,** gathered men of all nations, climes and peoples. The representatives of England and the nations on the continent of Europe, with the olive-colored children of the Asiatic races, here met the men of all the States of the American Union, in one wild, selfish scramble for gold.[2]

Arrival at San Francisco

The pen of man has not, as yet, realistically portrayed the miseries, the anguish and agonies of men as they suffered and struggled and died in huts, hovels, and on the damp, bare earth, by the thousands, in the old placer mines of this State. There are many men here who witnessed those scenes of almost unparalleled human suffering, and they speak of them even now with bated breath. Those who came by sea, and the Isthmus, on reaching **San Francisco**, found themselves **two hundred miles** away **from** the **gold-fields**, with the **Valley of the Sacramento**, one hundred miles across, lying between, and, during the Spring, flooded with the waste waters of the river, and in summer, steaming with deadly malarial disease. These obstacles were utterly disregarded, and thousands of young men, tenderly reared and highly educated, threw away their baggage and started on foot to the field of untold riches,

San Francisco, Winter of 1849. From, F. Marryat's Mountains and Molehills.
Courtesy of California State Library.

where they expected to realize that for which, amid the dangers of the sea, they had longed, and of which they had dreamed so fervently.

In the rallying of **Christendom to rescue the tomb of the Redeemer** from the possession of the Saracen, there was something that stirred the highest, the best, the **holiest attributes** of humanity; but in the meeting of nations to the "golden" sands of California, there was naught but greed for gain, with unutterable selfishness impelling all. Men forgot home, happiness and heaven; forgot the training of child-hood, manhood, and the fear of God. They madly threw all their past life to the four winds, and literally **changed the words of Holy Writ** and the highest maxims of human morality, and declared in every act, that "the love of money was the best policy, and honesty the root of all evil.[3]

Right and Honorable Exceptions

Still there were right and honorable exceptions to this abandonment of all the restraints of the soberer rules of life and the moral teachings of the past. In early days there came here **men who rose above the glitter and glamour of gold**; men who brought with them the unconquerable, undying belief that the "wealth of Ormus or of Ind" is not to be compared for a single moment to the glories that flame forever along the gold-paved streets of the New Jerusalem, and the **joys** that **await the toil-worn, faithful ones** in the **"city which hath foundations whose builder and maker is God"** – men who believed in the unrevealed glories and inex-haustible wealth to which holy men and women are heirs, beyond the sorrows, the sufferings, the evils, the disappointments and heart-breakings of this sin-stricken earth on which we pass an allotted pilgrimage. May we commemorate these dis-ciples of the Redeemer, who have passed to the "shining shore," and in honor of the few who yet remain and wait, ready to pass up and become heirs to an inheritance whose scenes of glory "surpass fable and are yet true scenes of accom-plished bliss?" These honorable exceptions laid the foundations for California.[4]

California's First Protestant Christian
Services – Prior to 1849

June 17, 1579: **Francis Drake** stepped ashore on Drake's Bay and one week later he held the **first Protestant Christian service** in English on the Pacific Coast. Before he departed on July 23 he erected "a great and firm post," to which he nailed a brass plate telling of his arrival and his claim to those lands in the name of his sovereign, Queen Elizabeth I.

1846: The **Rev. Walter Colton**, a Congregational minister, was chaplain on the frigate *Congress,* which spent the summer and fall of the year in the harbor of Monterey. He held services alternate Sundays on the frigates *Congress* and

PUBLISHED BY CHARLES P. KIMBALL, NOISY CARRIER'S PUBLISHING HALL.

Sample of a Printed Lettersheet, 1850's.
Courtesy of California State Library.

Savannah, and in 1847 there is a record of a Christian Revival among the seamen on these vessels. An article entitled *"Revival in the Navy"* appearing in the *New York Journal of Commerce*, reads as follows: Rev. Mr. Colton, chaplain of the U.S. frigate *Congress*, in a recent letter from Monterey, Ca. says: 'There is a deep interest among a large section of our crew on the subject of religion. It commenced two months back in my Bible class, and extended to others. I now hold a prayer meeting three evenings in the week, in a retired and very convenient apartment of our ship, and usually meet there about sixty sailors – about thirty of them have been hopefully pious. I invite them to pray and speak to the others, which they do with great fervency. Among the converts are some of the best seamen in our ship. Several of the officers have attended our meetings and we have no opposition from any quarter. This is all the work of a good Spirit, and I pray he may remain among us. I am the **only chaplain** out here, and officiate alternatively on board the frigates *Congress* and *Savannah*.'

At this time, **Mr. Colton** did not know of the presence of another Protestant Christian minister within the limits of the State. He was useful to the people of the State in many ways. In *1846*, Commander Stockton appointed him the first *Alcalde* of Monterey under the American flag. It was the policy of the American government of occupation at this time, to preserve as far as possible, the forms of the Mexican administration. But manifestly, in the interest of justice, some of these required modification. It was Mr. Colton who introduced for the first time, within the limits of the State, trial by jury.[5]

On August 15, 1846, Rev. Colton established the **first newspaper** in California. He found at Monterey an old press and type that had been used by a pastor for printing tracts and with these he issued *The Californian*. It was printed in Spanish and English and given an eager welcome by the community. Thus, Mr. Colton has the honor of planting some fundamental American institutions in the new territory. It was he who, as correspondent of the *Journal of Commerce* in New York, gave to the east its first knowledge of the discovery of gold in California. But so far as the Protestant Christian services were concerned, he seems to have confined these to the Navy and not to have held a service on shore.[6]

July 9, 1846: Captain John B. Montgomery, of the *Portsmouth,* raised the American flag over the Presidio of San Francisco. He was a **Presbyterian elder** and a profound Christian; and having no chaplain on board, he himself conducted church services on his vessel. The Sunday following the raising of the flag over the Plaza at Yerba Buena, on July 12th, Captain Montgomery went ashore with some of his men and conducted what was the first Protestant service on California soil after the raising of the U.S. flag. The **Rev. Sylvester Woodbridge, Jr.** (founder of the First Presbyterian Church of Benicia, on April 17, 1849) said: "…that noble, glorious gentleman, Captain Montgomery, came here in his sloop-of-war,

Portsmouth. He went ashore and enquired of the means of grace. Nothing of the kind was found. "Well," said he, "I will be preacher; I will perform those duties. We will have services every Sunday." Hence, during his stay in San Francisco harbor, these were the first Protestant Christian services held on shore under the American flag in California. The Plaza was renamed **Portsmouth Square** after his vessel, and **Montgomery Street** was named after Captain Montgomery.[7]

January 28, 1847: Lieutenant Theodorus Bailey commanding, the United States ship *Lexington* arrived in Monterey with a large box of the publications of the **American Tract Society**, which were distributed in the port.

1847: The captain of a certain whaling ship invited the **Rev. James C. Damon** to preach on board his vessel, as related by James Woods in his *California Pioneer Decade.*

April 25, 1847: The Rev. William Roberts, newly appointed Superintendent of Missions for Oregon, of the Methodist Episcopal Church, stopped on his way to preach in San Francisco. On the following Sunday, the **Rev. J.H. Wilbur**, his companion in travel, organized a **Sunday School** and **Bible Class** – but of short duration.

October, 1847: Rev. Elihu Anthony, a local preacher of the Methodist Episcopal Church, conducted a class in San José for two or three months.

1848: Mr. Anthony organized a class in Santa Cruz, which subsequently grew into the Methodist Church of that city. Rev. Anthony also preached occasionally in San Francisco during that year.

July 2, 1848: An extract from the diary of C.S. Lyman is related in an issue of the *California Historical Society Quarterly*, as follows: "**Sutter's Mill**: Mr. Douglass (his partner) and myself went to **Jones' Camp**, one and a half miles away, to engage in religious exercises. Most of the party belonging to his Camp were absent and it was concluded to appoint a religious meeting there for the next Sabbath." Also recorded – **July 30, 1848:** "Spent the day in camp. Mr. Matthews and son, and the Rev. Mr. Anthony came and spent the Sabbath with us and had religious exercises. Agreeable and profitable."[8]

Thus it is evident that **local Methodist preachers** performed a very real service in California before there was any regular ministrations of Protestant Christianity in the State.

October, 1848: Captain Lewis H. Thomas, of the English brig *Laura Ann,* held services of the English Protestant Church on shore in San Francisco.[9]

October 29, 1848: To the **Rev. T. Dwight Hunt, D.D.** belongs the honor of being the first Presbyterian minister to engage in Christian work in California. Prior to his arrival in San Francisco, he was pastor of the *American Church in Honolulu.* He had gone to the Sandwich Islands in 1844 as a missionary of the *American Board of Commissioners of Foreign Missions.* Here, in 1848, he had been invited by the Americans resident in Honolulu to build up a church among them. But when news of the discovery of gold in California reached the Islands, every foreigner who could get away started for the new territory. Mr. Hunt's congregation being thus naturally dissolved, he "obtained a leave of absence for three months, with the privilege of continued absence or return, as Providence should indicate" and set out with the rest of Honolulu for San Francisco. There was some question as to whether the recklessly wicked population would tolerate the presence of **a Protestant Christian minister.**[10]

Only one passion possessed the soul of the place – "gold" – which, whether gratified or ungratified, became the root of all evil. But he tells us himself that the very wickedness of the town at the time of his arrival had provoked a reaction which made even some of the godless ones long for the presence of a minister. Imagine then his astonishment when he found himself received with open arms and great enthusiasm. In **December, 1848, he became Chaplain-at-large to San Francisco**, at the same time deciding not to organize a church which would belong to any one denomination, for the space of one year. Three days later, Mr. Hunt was formally invited by the citizens, regardless of denominational affiliations, to make his home with them. He was elected *Protestant Chaplain of San Francisco*, and was voted a salary of $2,500.00 payable quarterly.

San Francisco, October 1848. Courtesy of California State Library.

View of San Francisco, formerly Yerba Buena, in 1846-7. Central Ship "A" is the Portsmouth – Captain John B. Montgomery, who raised the American flag over the Presidio in San Francisco, aboard.

The public school house on the Plaza was voted by the town for his use on Sundays and formal announcement was made that he would hold services twice on Sundays – at 11:00 a.m. and 7:30 p.m. The attendance, however, was far too great for the accommodations which the school house afforded, and the congregation crowded the doors and windows at each service.[11]

The Lord's Supper –
First Protestant Service in California

January, 1849: It is recorded of Mr. Hunt's work, that on the **first Sunday in January, 1849,** he administered the **Lord's Supper** for the first time at a Protestant Christian Service in California and had twelve communicants who represented six different denominations. Until the arrival of the *California,* February 28, 1849, Mr. Hunt was the **only Protestant minister in California**!

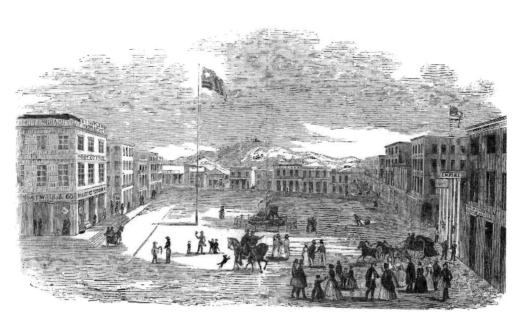

View of the Grand Plaza or Public Square, San Francisco, 1849.
Courtesy of California State Library.

CHAPTER VII

Four Pioneer Founders on the *"California"*
February 28, 1849

The first ministers of the Gospel who came here to plant **Christian Protestantism** on the ruins of the Catholic Missions of three quarters of a century gone by, were four in number. They came together on the same ship. Three of them came out under the patronage of the *American Home Missionary Society.* They were, Rev. S.H. Willey, D.D.; Rev. Sylvester Woodbridge, Jr. and Rev. J.W. Douglas. The fourth, Rev. Osgood C. Wheeler, D.D., came under the patronage of the *American Baptist Home Mission Society.* Of the four, **Rev. Samuel Hopkins Willey**, the *Congregational minister*, became widely known as the first Chaplain of the Constitutional Convention and settled at Monterey, then the Capital of the State. In his *Colton Hall Recollections*, Rev. Willey gives us this account:

> **Some recollections of Colton Hall** by Rev. S.H. Willey, D.D., a Chaplain of the Constitutional Convention held there in September, 1849:
>
> On landing in Monterey from the Pacific Mail Steamship *California* on February 28, 1849, I found a thoroughly Mexican town in every respect. There was but one style of architecture after which all buildings were patterned. But there was one exception.
>
> On the side hill, a little back of town, stood a new, two-story stone building, that looked as if it might have dropped down from a New England village. There was no other building to be seen that resembled it, and I was not long in going to see what it was for. I found it entirely completed, all its rooms and passage-ways were finished. There were two large square rooms on the first floor, and one great hall occupied all the space on the second floor.

The Pacific Mail Steamship, "California."
First Steamship to enter the Golden Gate.

*Colton Hall, Monterey. Site of the California Constitutional
Convention, September, 1849.*

There was nobody about the building. In the hall were some carpenters' tools, saws, planes, hammers, chisels, etc., and some bits of lumber scattered about as if the owners had left hastily. And this, I afterwards learned, had been the case. On the discovery of gold on the American River, carpenters were in as much haste as other people to get to the mines, and lost no time in caring for tools. So there they were, just as the owners had dropped them.

In this condition **Colton Hall** stood during the summer, except that a **school** of some **sixty boys and girls** was gathered and taught in one of the lower rooms during that time.

Meanwhile things were exceedingly quiet in Monterey, for men were in the mines, and only women and children were at home, save that the officers of the government were there attending to their duties. These consisted largely in sending out horseback expresses and receiving them in return, preparatory to the assembling of the **first Constitutional Convention in California**, which was called to meet in **Colton Hall** on the 1st of September, 1849.

The peculiar circumstances under which that convention was called, and the excellence and critical importance of the work done there have lent a dignity to the building itself, suggesting that it should be preserved.

It was undoubtedly the most suitable place for a convention in California at that time. It was built of white stone quarried from a neighboring hill. The large hall in the second story was seventy feet long by thirty feet wide. It was reached by a wide stairway from the rear of the building. The front of the building was ornamented with a portico which you entered from the hall, and was supported by two lofty pillars.

When the time came for the meeting of the convention, carpenters were employed to put the hall in readiness for its use. Some three-fourths of the length of the hall was divided off by a rail for the exclusive use of the members, and the rest was left for spectators.

A raised platform was placed at the end of the hall for **the President**, and tables in front of it for the **secretaries and clerks**. Chairs were placed on either side of the central space in front of the President to accommodate the **forty-eight members**.

The sessions of the convention opened on Monday, September 3rd. **Robert Semple** was chosen **President** and took the chair, and **William G. Marcy** was made **secretary.** The **half dozen native Californians** were assigned chairs near together, and **their interpreter** sat with them. The other members took seats as it happened, for they were nearly all strangers to each other, meeting now for the first time. The seats first taken were usually retained through the session.

On the President's right, I remember sat Francis J. Lippitt, Edward Gilbert, W.M. Gwin and others, and on his left H.W. Halleck, Myron Norton, T.O. Larkin, M.G. Vallejo, J.R. Snyder and others not now called.

For over one month **that hall** was the **scene of most earnest and critically important work**, and the results of it are seen in **the history of the State** and of **the nation** ever since.[1]

> In retrospect, thirty years later, **Rev. Dr. Samuel Hopkins Willey** wrote in his book, *Thirty Years in California:*
>
> Thirty years ago I was thinking "what shall be my theme for my first sermon in California?" I was on the steamship which had then just anchored in the harbor of Monterey; I could not at once find a place to stay on shore. It was Saturday, and I was to **preach the next day in Colton Hall**. I remained on shipboard to prepare. "What shall be my text?" thought I. "It shall be one that most clearly expressed my errand here," I said to myself; and so I thought – "We preach Christ, the power of God, and the wisdom of God," – that is my errand, and that shall be my text; and I would take the same text, and let it express the same errand again now.
>
> That day I had to prepare my discourse on the deck of the steamship. It was the quietest place I could find; and even there I had to cling close to the capstan, sitting beside it on a camp stool, in order not to be pushed about in the general rush. But the noise did not concern me, and therefore it did not disturb me. **I was at last in California.** Those circling hills around Monterey were beautiful after the winter rains, as they are now. There was inspiration in the air, in the landscape, in the occasion, in the theme, in

everything. And now, after the period of a generation has passed away, there is no theme more fitting to the changed situation than this same theme.

As I prepared my anniversary discourse upon it this year, it was not on a ship's deck, amid the rush of gold-seekers just arrived in the golden land, looking forward to a State yet to be, but it was in my own quiet study, surrounded by my books, and all the needed appliances and helps in my work. I prepared it to be preached, not in a half-finished, unfurnished room, to a small assembly of men, but in a comely and convenient church, to a congregation representing homes, and a well-ordered Christian society. A church which is **one of 600 or 700 Protestant churches**, where **then there was not one of any denomination**. The preaching of that theme seemed to me, in the beginning, worthy of devotion of the noblest life, and it appears to me today, more surpassingly so than it did then. The study of these years, the experience of these years, the living and dying, raise it, in my view, to a higher esteem than ever. And not less does the personal experiences through all these years, in joy and in sorrow, in health and in sickness, in safety and in danger, lead me to rank this theme as the one of absolutely supreme moment today. With it, I began my ministry, and with it I would now begin it anew, thankful for the undiminished health and strength that permits me to do so. And as long as I live, and in every way in which I am able, I will preach *"Christ and Him crucified, the power of God and the wisdom of God."*[2]

On the *"California"* in Monterey Bay
February 28, 1849

As for going on to **the gold mines**, "Who can reconcile gold-digging with the proper objects of the Christian ministry?" asked Willey. "Of what value would it be to preach the gospel to men who were seeking not truth but gold?" Looking towards the placers, Protestant missionaries were appalled by what seemed a nightmare of drunkenness, gambling, materialism, and disdain for religious principles. "The Americans," wrote an observer, "think only of dollars, talk only of dollars, seek nothing but dollars; they are the men of dollars." But religion in the gold field, as it turned out, was not so anomalous as it seemed. In all of the major towns and many of the minor ones, congregations were organized and churches built, even though they were small congregations and, for the most part, modest churches. For all its iniquity in the eyes of the missionaries, gold-rush society contained men and women, as Willey discovered, who were "...ready to enter heartily into the work of establishing the institutions of the Gospel."[3]

Rev. Willey also served as ***chaplain at the Presidio***. Convinced that teaching should be as potent as preaching, he launched a ***public school***, serving as ***pioneer teacher***. He also gathered $1,500 and founded the ***first library in California***. Meanwhile, he preached in Monterey's Colton Hall. Removing to San Francisco in March of 1850, he organized the ***Howard Presbyterian Church***.

The Presidio Chapel, San Francisco, California.
Courtesy of California State Library.

San Francisco's First Admission Day Parade – September 29, 1850 –
Courtesy of California State Library.

College of California, Oakland. Courtesy of California State Library.

Willey – Founder of The College of California

At the same time, Rev. Willey intensified his efforts to give California youth the educational privileges given him at **Dartmouth College** in Hanover, New Hampshire. He raised $3,000 to help **Henry Durant** create the **College School in Oakland** in 1854. Then he enlisted **Frederick Billings** in the Oakland project. Billings was later the financier of the Northern Pacific Railroad. His wife was the granddaughter of the sister of Eleazar Wheelock, founder of Dartmouth in 1769. By 1859 the College School in Oakland became known as the **College of California** with Billings as Chairman and Rev. Willey as Secretary. It was not until April 16, 1860 that a new site for the school was dedicated in Berkeley. **Rev. Samuel Hopkins Willey** was acting president of the college during 1862-69, when it was accepted by the California Board of Regents to become the central root of the **University of California**.[4]

The Presbyterian missionaries on board the **California** were **Rev. Sylvester Woodbridge, Jr.,** who proceeded to Benicia, organizing the first church body in the State, and **Rev. J.W. Douglas**, who began his labors at San José, subsequently founding the first religious paper in California – **The Pacific**.

Rev. Osgood C. Wheeler, a Baptist minister, also on the **California**, proceeded to Yerba Buena, (now San Francisco) beside the Golden Gate, a city of tents, shacks, over the hills and close to the waterfront; a city with more saloons and gambling houses than family homes. There was at the time, no Protestant Christian church in the whole of California.[5]

In an article entitled, **First Steamship Pioneers** we read of their arrival on the *California*:

> The 1,100-ton Pacific mail steamer, **California** rounded Point Pinos, her sidewheel paddles plunging rhythmically into the calm waters of Monterey Bay…As the *California* approached the shore, her 365 passengers stood on the deck, eagerly looking shoreward for a glimpse of the buildings and homes of Monterey, then the Capital of the land to which they had sailed in search of gold.

> All at once, through the late morning mist, they saw the American flag waving from the Custom House flagpole. A spontaneous cheer broke from their lips. On shore, a cannon of the Presidio battery began firing an 18-gun salute…

> Thus to the shores of California came the first American steamer that ever sailed the Pacific, and the **'49ers of the great California Gold**

First Baptist Church, San Francisco. The First Free Public School in California met here. Courtesy of California State Library.

Mission St.

Rush...When she was two months out and thousands of miles at sea, **President Polk**, in Washington, published the news that gold had been discovered in the valley of **Coloma,** three thousand miles west in California.[6]

San Francisco in 1849

Here is **Dr. Samuel Hopkins Willey's** description of San Francisco in 1849:

Passing back from the wharf a short distance, we came upon buildings erected for hotels, dwelling houses, etc. They go up as it were in an hour with a rapidity really astonishing. They are brought ashore from vessels, all ready to put together and are very quickly filled with dwellers paying rent up to $30,000 a year. Still farther back are tents – so numerous they resemble an army encampment. These pay ground rent.

I saw one put up not more than 10 feet square on an open lot, for which lot the owner of the tent was to pay $100.00 a month ground rent. The **rush of business** is truly wonderful. Everybody is busy – so much so that it seems as if a man who stops to answer a question in monosyllables felt as if he was losing five dollars out of his pocket.

Many are making money at a most rapid rate. Some few who have over-traded are ready to fail. Another class is becoming very numerous – young men who have got the fever or some other disease and have just means enough to get down to this town and are out of health and of funds, out of spirits and dreadfully homesick.

Gambling houses pay the highest rents and this keeps all rents high. Some young mechanics of my acquaintance have just erected one of the finest and well adapted for any business, and have rented it to a gambling company for $35,000.00 a year – no other business will pay so well. This vice is rife here. Every night the rooms are open in all parts of town - with the glare of lights, the chink of money and the cheer of music. A bar, of course, is a necessary appendix.[7]

Sunday Morning in the Mines, 1872. Painting by Charles Christian Nahl.
Courtesy of the Crocker Art Museum.

Crocker Art Library, Sacramento

An Urgent Need of Religious and Educational Workers

Dr. Willey's letter went on to show the urgent need of religious and educational workers from the East. Telling about **Sacramento**, he wrote:

> Three months ago there were but few houses, only four or five, and now it is thickly settled over a large area, and is growing amazingly. They talk about twelve or fourteen thousand people there; but it is **another San Francisco**, repeated again, only the growth has been three times as rapid. All is orderly, law-abiding. Gamblers are numerous, but public sentiment is against them and when combined and a little more accentuated, it will frown them into secrecy. This is evident from what is now.[8]

It is a notable fact that in detailing the early history of California, after the advent of the Americans, historians give us the details of the lawlessness that prevailed; of the gambling, the robberies and murders which led to the formation of the **Vigilante**, but rarely, very rarely, is a word said about the religious and moral atmosphere of the new communities. It is true that a well-known artist of early California, Charles Christian Nahl, painted *A Sunday Morning in the Mines*, in which we see to the right, under a hut awning, a man reading his Bible. However, the central figure is a drunken miner throwing his gold dust to the winds – a shooting affair over a card game is to his left. Yet, as we have already seen, from the earliest arrivals with **the Gold Rush**, there were **ministers of the Gospel** representing various denominations, and a decided respect for men of the cloth.[9]

San Francisco's First Baptist Church
August 5, 1849

Amidst the wickedness and vice that predominated in San Francisco in 1849, the First Baptist Church of San Francisco was born. At the close of the war with Mexico, in which California was ceded to the United States, the *Board of the Home Mission Society* decided that it "should establish a Mission in California." They selected San Francisco as its most favorable place. A young man, they believed, who was full of zeal for his Lord should be sent on this mission. There was just such a young man, in his first pastorate at Jersey City, New Jersey, who was asked by **Dr. B.M. Hill**, *Corresponding Secretary of the Home Mission Society,* "to go to California as our pioneer missionary." **Rev. Osgood Wheeler** was too dumbfounded to answer this proposal. Rev. Wheeler argued long and earnestly against this mission, no one being able to change his mind. After sixteen days of arguments – for and against – Rev. Wheeler and his wife spent a night on their knees in prayer, beseeching the Lord to guide them. At the close of morning devotions, they rose to their feet and began to sing: "To God I'm reconciled; His pardoning voice I hear;

First Presbyterian Church, San Francisco.
Organized May 20, 1849.

First Baptist Church, San Francisco.
First Protestant Church in California, 1849.

He owns me for his child, I will no longer fear." Rev. Wheeler felt that "a burden like that which rolled from the shoulders of **John Bunyan**" had been removed from his shoulders. They knew they were obeying God's call to go to **California – "the darkest mission field"** as it was then called.[10]

The Wheelers left on the steamer *Falcon* for the Isthmus of Panama. Three days later, news of the **discovery of gold reached Washington.** Their trip was "full of hazards." When they reached Cruces, a vast multitude had collected, following the discovery of gold. Cholera broke out. After twenty-five miles to Panama via bridle paths, over almost impassable streams and mountains, another fourteen days elapsed before the steamer *California* reached port. Arriving in San Francisco on February 28, 1849, the *California* was the first steamer to enter the Golden Gate. It took the Wheelers ninety days to reach their destination.

Rev. Wheeler wrote that, "the religion then dominant in the country was in its most dilapidated state and lowest form of superstition." He also noted that, "between the 1st of April and 1st of August, 1849, forty-six Baptists who claimed to be ministers arrived in San Francisco – all of them continuing to the gold mines." Not one of them stopped for a single day to help him. However, Rev. Wheeler was more interested in **"God's rush to California"** than the "rush for gold" which was the downfall of many.

Shortly after his arrival in San Francisco, **Rev. Wheeler** organized the **first Baptist Church in San Francisco**, on Washington Street (between Dupont and Stockton) – now, the heart of Chinatown. **Dedicated on August 5, 1849**, it was the first building devoted entirely to Protestant Christian purposes in the Bay City. A simple frame building thirty by fifty feet, costing $6,000.00, it was the **first Protestant Christian church building** ever constructed **in California**. Preceding the church's dedication, at the end of **May, 1849, a Sunday school** was started.[11]

The first Free Public School in California was organized and held here from December 26, 1849 – June 22, 1851.

By 1850, **Rev. Osgood Wheeler** had established churches in Sacramento and San José, with a combined membership of 53.

**San Francisco's First Presbyterian
Church came via Cape Horn**

In **April, 1849**, a few weeks after the arrival of the *California,* **Rev. Albert Williams** came to San Francisco, organizing the *First Presbyterian Church* there on May 20, 1849. He also opened a **Sunday school** and a **Day school**. From **August 18, 1849 – January 19, 1851**, the congregation met in **a tent** on Dupont Street, now Grant

First Congregational Church, San Francisco.
"The Old Schoolhouse on the Plaza" in which the first services were held.

TRINITY C^H PINE STREET

Trinity Episcopal Church, San Francisco.

Avenue, between Pacific and Broadway. The tent-church accommdated 200 persons.

Later, building material was ordered from New York and came by ship, including a pulpit, lamps, seats and a bell. This first church was 35 feet wide and 75 feet long and could seat 800 people. It took over a year for the church to make the journey via Cape Horn, and it was not ready for occupancy until January, 1851. It may be interesting to add that, set up and ready for use in San Francisco, the church cost $16,000.00.[12]

An article entitled, "*A Beautiful Anniversary*" celebrating the First Presbyterian Church, San Francisco's nineteenth year, discloses that, "**The first Presbyterian Sunday school in San Francisco** is one of the oldest in the city. In those early days of '49, it was organized as a little leaven in the midst of a great mass of wickedness, and though it has not exactly 'leavened the whole lump,' it has done not a little towards it. **The school** met at first in **a tent**, and for a good many years was small and struggling, but during a long time now, it has been very flourishing..."[13]

San Francisco's First
Congregational Church

July 29, 1849: On the morning of Sunday, July 29, 1849, a meeting was held in the **school house** located on the Plaza of San Francisco, to consider the advisability of organizing a *Congregational Church*. Frederick S. Hawley was elected chairman, and George N. Seymour secretary. The meeting was opened with prayer. After discussion it was voted on motion of Mr. Thomas Douglass that the following letter be addressed to **Rev. T. Dwight Hunt,** who was the first Protestant clergyman located as such in California, and was then acting as the chaplain of the town:

> Rev. T. Dwight Hunt:
> Dear Brother:
>
> We, the undersigned, adopting as our standard of doctrine and government the articles of faith and the forms now in use in the evangelical *Congregational churches* in New England, request you to organize us into a church, to be called *"The First Congregational Church of San Francisco."* (Signed – 10 persons)

On the afternoon of the same day, eight persons were organized into "The First Congregational Church of San Francisco," and Rev. T. Dwight Hunt was invited to act as stated above. Thomas Douglass and Frederick S. Hawley were elected Deacons.[14]

The school house was secured for afternoon services, it being occupied morning and evening by **Mr. Hunt as Chaplain**. On the following Sabbath, the Deacons were ordained, and the sacrament of the Lord's Supper was administered, **Rev. Albert Williams** of the *First Presbyterian Church* assisting. Steps were at once taken to provide a suitable place of worship, and on February 10th, 1850, a building was dedicated to the worship of God; this building was 25 by 50 feet in size, and was located at the corner of Jackson and Virginia Streets. On the 26th March, 1850, a call, which was accepted, was extended to Mr. Hunt to become the Pastor of the Church. The Council convened to install Mr. Hunt, met on June 26th and was composed of the following persons: Rev. J.A. Benton, First Church of Christ, Sacramento; Rev. S.V. Blakeslee, Marysville, and Rev. Samuel Hopkins Willey, Monterey. *Order of Service*: Invocation and Reading of Scripture – *Rev. S.V. Blakeslee*. Sermon: *Rev. J.A. Benton*. Installing Prayer: *Rev. S.H. Willey*. Charge to the Pastor and Right Hand of Fellowship: *Rev. Osgood C. Wheeler* of the *First Baptist Church*. Charge to the People: *Rev. S.H. Willey.*[15]

In the summer of 1852 arrangements were made for the erection of a brick edifice on the corner of California and Dupont Streets, and the building was dedicated July 10, 1853. At the close of 1854, Mr. Hunt resigned the pastorate, and delivered the farewell sermon on the first Sabbath in January, 1855. During this year the pulpit was filled by *Rev. I.H. Brayton*. The pulpit was occupied the early part of 1856 by *Rev. Edward S. Lacy*, and June 4th, a call was voted for him to become pastor. This call was accepted, and the installing council met July 5th, composed of the following persons: *Rev. Horace Bushnell, D.D*. of Hartford, Connecticut; *Rev. Samuel Hopkins Willey, Rev. I.H. Brayton* and *Rev. J.E. Benton*, all of San Francisco; Rev. A.A. Baker of Petaluma, and Mr. S.W. Brown, delegate from the Church in Petaluma. Rev. S.H. Willey was Moderator, and Rev. S.A. Baker, Scribe. The order of service was as follows: Invocation and Reading of Scripture, *Rev. J.E. Benton*. Installing Prayer, *Rev. S.H. Willey*. Sermon, *Rev. Horace Bushnell, D.D*. Charge to the Pastor, *Rev. T. Dwight Hunt*. Right Hand of Fellowship, *Rev. A.A. Baker*. Charge to the People, *Rev. I.H. Brayton*. Benediction, *Rev. E.S. Lacy*.

The pastorate of *Rev. Lacy* was one of great spiritual power, and his influence over the young men of the congregation was most remarkable.[16]

San Francisco's First Episcopal Church

1849: Rev. Flavel Scott Mines, an Episcopal minister, came to this coast, and organized a church under the name *Trinity Church*, on **July 17, 1849**. It stood on Pine Street (between Montgomery and Kearney) where the California market now stands. It was the *first Episcopal Church on the Pacific Coast* and the second Protestant Christian church west of the Rocky Mountains.[17]

1849: *Grace Parish* was organized by Episcopal minister, **Rev. Dr. John Leno Ver Mehr.** The founder of *Grace Parish* was born in Namur, Belgium in 1809. Scholarly and spiritual, rather than worldly and practical, his was a personal and spiritual quest beset by many obstacles to overcome. After a youth spent as a political outcast with his father, brilliant success at Leiden University, Holland, a restless period as a tutor, and success at founding his own school, he turned to Christianity as the only Truth in life. In 1846 he emigrated to New York where he came under the teaching of Bishop G.W. Doane of New Jersey, becoming a deacon in 1846 and pastor in 1847. In 1848 he was appointed as the *first Episcopal missionary to California.*[18]

The appointment of **Rev. Ver Mehr** to the missionary field in California was the result of a request from a group of churchmen in San Francisco who promised "full support and aid" to the missionary chosen by the Board of Missions. He was about to leave when struck down by a nearly fatal attack of smallpox. A second group of San Francisco churchmen, impatient at the delay, wrote to various Eastern clergy asking for a missionary. The **Rev. Flavel Mines** was chosen, with the Board's <u>unofficial</u> blessing, and sent via Panama. His faith undeterred, however, **Rev. Ver Mehr** set out in the summer of 1849. Sailing via Cape Horn, he arrived in San Francisco on September 8, 1849. The two ministers met, and soon became fast friends.[19]

A small chapel was built at Powell and John Streets, near Jackson Street in the winter of 1849. The little barn-like shingle-roofed chapel was the sixth church building in the city and became the third Episcopal parish in the West. The name *Grace Chapel* was chosen by Dr. Ver Mehr in reference to Rev. Mines' *Trinity* Church, and the two main New York parishes of the time – *Trinity* and *Grace.* Seating 240 people, the chapel had wooden benches and canvas partitions forming the vestry. *The first service took place December 30, 1849.* Dr. Ver Mehr writes: "I peeped through the canvas partition. Sturdy miners came in and took their seats on the rough planks, taking up the prayer-books and evidently in earnest. Others came. A few ladies, very few." He continues, "The responses were loud and clear. My first sermon listened to with attention…The plates went round. There was not one silver piece on them! I had nothing but gold to offer at the altar." The first Communion service was celebrated the following Sunday. Gamblers were audible nearby. The city's first major fire had destroyed much of the district and the gamblers had set up tables in the blackened ruins! However, God blessed the service – all those in attendance leaving spiritually revived. A new *Grace Chapel* building was opened for service on July 19, 1851. **The first Oratorio** – "Stabat Mater" - ever given in San Francisco, was sung at a sacred concert given to defray expenses of the building.[20]

Grace Episcopal Church,
Powell, between Pacific and Jackson Streets, San Francisco.

Grace Chapel, Nob Hill, San Francisco.

The Chinese Mission – results of Rev. Ver Mehr's pioneer missionary work: On the evening of Easter Tuesday, 1906, the Easter festival for the Chinese Mission was held in the church basement. Bibles were distributed and the meeting closed with Hymn 415, containing the words – "Cover my defenceless head with the shadow of Thy wing." This was to be the last service held at *Grace Church*. At 5:12 a.m. the following morning, a tremendous earthquake, of 8.3 magnitude, shook San Francisco. At 5:45 the rector, the Rev. David J. Evans, inspected the church and found only minor damage. Many gable tops were destroyed. Not a window, however, was broken. There seemed little cause for alarm. By late afternoon, Easter Wednesday, fires in the downtown area became uncontrollable, the conflagration beginning to climb Nob Hill. Rev. Evans quickly salvaged most of the parish records, struggling across Nob Hill with his family. A few minutes after 2 a.m. on Maundy Thursday, *Grace Church* burned. At dawn, the "Old Warder of the Hill" was in ruins. As Rev. Evans prepared to board a ferry to Alameda on the day after the fire, he met one of his **Chinese** pupils, **a little girl**, **"Ah May,"** *her new Bible still clutched tightly in her hands.*[21]

Through the munificence of **the Crocker family**, their property near the summit of Nob Hill, with its two ruined mansions, was given for a cathedral site in June, 1906. Bishop Nichols notes propitiously that "**Nob**" was also a city of priests near Jerusalem (I Samuel 21-22). The proximity of old *Grace Church* with its cathedral aspirations, resulted in its eventual transition to *Grace Cathedral*. For the next seven years, however, the parish worshiped in a little wood and shingle church at the northeast corner of the future cathedral close. One of the treasured items from old *Grace Church* was the marble in the Ebenezer Altar. The three panels were of marble salvaged from the ruins by Bishop Nichols. The left panel read: *"After the earthquake, a fire, after the fire, a still small voice." (I Kings 19:21).* The Service and Consecration of the new *Grace Cathedral,* with its tower and carillon of bells – the dream, and gift – of Dr. N.T. Coulson, took place on November 20, 1964.[22]

Rev. Dr. Ver Mehr would be awed and amazed at the results of his **pioneer work** – a great cathedral rising majestically near the hilltop.

San Francisco's First Methodist Church

On October 8, 1849, the First Methodist Church was dedicated.

In 1847, *The Baltimore General Conference of the Methodist Church* appointed the **Rev. William Roberts** to do mission work in Yerba Buena (now San Francisco). On Sunday, **April 25, 1847**, he conducted the **first Methodist service** ever held in San Francisco. The Methodist community grew rapidly in California and the first Methodist house of worship, known as the "Shanty with the Blue

First Methodist Church, San Francisco. Dedicated, October 8, 1849.

Cover," was the home of Asa White, a preacher from Oregon who moved his family to California. This very rustic house of worship was later officially recognized by Rev. Roberts as First Methodist Church.[23]

The **Rev. William Taylor**, the first ordained minister to San Francisco, came to the Bay City in 1849 and assisted Rev. Roberts in the construction of the new church, by rowing across the Bay to Oakland to cut timber for the church. The new **"First Church"** completed and dedicated on **October 8, 1849,** was located at Washington and Powell Streets.

The **Rev. Isaac Owen** and **Rev. William Taylor** gathered *Methodist* congregations in San Francisco. The Methodists established **"Seamen's Bethel,"** which was especially devoted to the sailors, of whom there was a great assortment from all parts of the world. The pastor of Bethel, **Rev. Taylor**, also delivered open-air addresses to large congregations every Sunday in *Portsmouth Square*, which had a good effect on the morals of the community.[24]

Many Christian organizations had their origin in *"First Church,"* including the **California Bible Society** (1849) and the **Methodist Book Concern** (1850). On **October 30, 1849,** the Methodists began holding meetings of **a Bible Society**.

Thus, **in 1849,** the five leading Christian Protestant denominations became, to some extent, organized in California.

Sacramento's First Protestant Churches
The First Baptist Church

After founding and establishing the *First Baptist Church* in San Francisco, **Rev. Osgood Wheeler** came to Sacramento on September 4, 1850, calling on **Judge E.J. Willis**, a lawyer and first Judge of Sacramento County Court of Sessions. Arrangements were made for the organization of a church there.

On September 14, 1850, the First Baptist Church of Sacramento was organized with **sixteen members**. This meeting took place in the Willis' home then located on H Street between Sixth and Seventh, where the Hall of Justice stands. On the following day, public worship services were held in the Court House, then located on I Street between Fourth and Fifth, **Rev. Wheeler** preaching the sermon of recognition. Meetings continued to be held in the Court House during the fall and winter of 1850, and in the Spring, 1851, the first baptism, that of J.L. Wadsworth, took place on October 6, 1860, being the **second recorded baptism** in the State of California – the first being in San Francisco, and the third in San José.[25]

Sacramento City, California, in 1849.
Courtesy of The Mariners' Museum.

First Baptist Church, Sacramento – First House of Worship,
1850. Seventh and L Streets.

In April, 1854, a second church edifice was begun on Fourth Street, between K and L Streets. It was eighty-five by thirty-five feet, with a vestry of thirty-two by fifteen feet. The auditorium seated five hundred. The cost was $9,000, including furniture, and at the time it was said to be the **"best Protestant church building in the State."** It was dedicated the last Sunday of June, 1854.[26]

Preachers in early California recognized newspapers as a means of outreach. On August 19, 1854, there began the publication of a weekly paper in Sacramento, **Rev. Wheeler and Judge Willis** being **editors.** This paper was known as the *Pacific Banner,* the first Baptist paper printed west of the Rockies. This newspaper was outspoken **in support of the Chinese.**[27]

Work Among the Chinese

In February, 1848, the **first Chinese** to arrive in modern California came on the Brig *"Eagle"* from **Hong Kong**. There were two men and one woman. However, with the discovery of gold, the influx of Chinese was so great that by May, 1852 there were about 12,000 men and two women. Long before this, however, there had been extensive trade carried on by American ships between California and China.

First Baptist Church, Sacramento – Second House of Worship, 1854.
Fourth, between K & L Streets.
Called "the best Protestant church building in the State."

Chinese Chapel, Sacramento, 1854. 6th and H Streets.

Chinese letter from Wong Min, Canton, China.

In their new environment, the Chinese found themselves seemingly only wanted as *"hewers of wood and drawers of water."* Miners were Caucasian men. The Chinese were not allowed to mine except in abandoned diggings. Christian people, however, had a different attitude toward them – these Chinese souls being precious in the sight of the Lord.

The first recorded work among the Chinese on the Pacific Coast was by Presbyterians in San Francisco in October, 1850. The Baptists' Christian outreach to them was in Sacramento in **1854** by **Rev. J.L. Shuck**. Rev. Shuck was a missionary under appointment of the Triennial Convention, which sent him as the first *American Baptist missionary to China* in September, 1835. Returning to Virginia in 1846, he contacted the *Southern Baptist Board*, which sent him back to China; and in the Spring of 1854, he was sent by them to the Pacific Coast to work among the Chinese.[28]

Arriving in San Francisco, the work there being already undertaken by the Presbyterians, he proceeded to Sacramento, where the First Baptist Church invited him to fill the pulpit until such time as they could secure a pastor. **Rev. Shuck was well versed** in the **Cantonese language**, and with the customs and habits of the Chinese people. Among the first fifteen Chinese to accept Christ as their Saviour and follow His example in baptism, was *"Ah Moay"* on April 21, 1854, who was given a license to preach on November 2, 1856. The church therefore has the distinction of having baptized the first Chinese believer, and of having given the first license to preach to a Chinese in America.

"Ah Moay" was a man of learning and ability. Associated with Rev. Shuck were three Chinese: *"Ah Chak,"* a man of attainment, business ability and influence; *"Wong Chong"* and *"Fong Fo,"* both of whom were active, fervent Christians. *"Leong Chak"* also assisted Rev. Shuck.[29]

On November 1, 1854, representing the Southern Baptist Convention, Rev. Shuck purchased a lot on the northwest corner of Sixth and H Streets for $300.00. *The Chinese Chapel* was dedicated on this site on June 10, 1854. This was the *first Chinese chapel* erected in America by the Baptists, the greater part of the funds coming from Virginia. Of interest historically, is that an African-American church – *Siloam Baptist Church*, held its first meeting in this chapel. In January, 1860, the fifteen Chinese members of First Baptist Church organized themselves in the *"Tseay Tih" Baptist Church*, **Rev. Shuck** acting as their first pastor.[30]

Of great historic interest, in connection with the First Baptist Church's outreach and *work among the Chinese*, is a letter written from Canton, China, dated November 19, 1866. It indicates that at least a second license to preach was given by the church to a Chinese, in addition to the one granted *"Ah Moay,"* as shown in the photograph. Its translation into English follows:

> **Wong Min**, a disciple of Jesus, writes this to the First Baptist Church at Sacramento. May our Heavenly Father bless you, Amen. I have been preaching ever since I left you and returned to China. When I was connected with your church ten years ago, Mr. Shuck and you, brethren and sisters, appointed me a preacher and gave me a paper as proof. During the typhoon several years ago, I lost everything and the certificate among the rest. I write this to ask the church to renew it. You will find it by reference to the church records; Mr. Spencer, the apothecary, Mr. and Mrs. Strong, who sold lacquer boxes; and Mrs. Haswell will remember it. We have heard that Mr. Shuck has died. Please let me know whether it is so or not. If he is living, ask him to come to China and preach for "the harvest is great and the labourers are few." I have also heard that my dear brother, Ngai A. Fak, died at the Silver Mines. Please let me know whether it is so or not. If Yeung A. Fo, Wong A. Tsung or Kook A. Tai return to China, ask them to come to my house. I am in Canton helping Pastor Graves to preach. May God bless you all. Amen.
>
> – Wong Min.[31]

Sacramento's Methodist Church
that came via Cape Horn

Sacramento also had a church that made a trip around the Horn. The *Methodists* appealed to their brethren in the East and the latter sent them the materials for the Church building that stood on 6th Street in the Capital city, until replaced by the present building erected on the same site.

In **April, 1849**, **Rev. W. Grove Deal**, a physician and local Methodist preacher, began holding Protestant services in Sacramento.[32]

Marysville's First Protestant
Christian Churches

The *Presbyterians* erected in Marysville a church which the late W. Mills, land agent of the Southern Pacific for many years, always declared was the most perfect piece of architecture in the State. He never visited Marysville without going to admire the tower and front of the edifice.[33]

The *Episcopalians* erected their first California church in Marysville also. Marysville, at the time that it became such a notable church center, was the starting point for numerous stage routes to the mines, and was as "wide open" as San Francisco.[34]

First Chinese Colony in California
– stage for Chinese Revolution

The First Chinese Colony in the State was also established in Marysville, the Chinese erecting their **first church** there. It was from that center that **"Sun Yet"** and other Americanized Chinese went forth to start the **revolution in China** that overthrew the dynasty and established the Republic.[35]

In Sacramento, Marysville and mining areas in the State, there were **Protestant Christian societies** which were all liberally supported and all seem to have had a large attendance.

October 17, 1850: Rev. Martin C. Briggs, entered the Golden Gate on the famous *SS Oregon*. Called the "*Methodist Trumpeter of California*" he served many terms in the Methodist Conference as pastor in leading San Francisco churches, and at Sacramento. One of his latest appointments was at Napa.

July 10, 1853: *The Young Men's Christian Association* began its work in San Francisco. Here is **Dr. Albert Williams'** account: "It was my privilege to be one of the founders of the YMCA in San Francisco. I was prompt to give the proposal of organization a special attention. The meeting...was held in the *First Presbyterian Church*, and the draft of a constitution was made by myself. At that meeting, July 18, 1853, the YMCA of San Francisco was formally instituted.

The **Pacific Tract Society** and a number of other church organizations were also begun.

Condition of Society in California

The condition of society in California in those days is conveyed by a French writer, describing a trip made across the Atlantic on an English ship. All week, he said, everybody was busy playing cards and gambling as if their lives depended upon winning. On Sunday, the cards had disappeared and he was astonished on attending Protestant services in the cabin, to see the most zealous gamblers leading the choir with several of their fellow card-players among the singers, and all singing the hymns with great zeal and enthusiasm.[36]

Sabbath in San Francisco – 1850

Another interesting article, appearing in the ***Daily Alta California's October 28, 1850*** Sunday edition, gives a newcomer's surprise at San Francisco on the Sabbath:

Sunday. – The newcomer in San Francisco is quite surprised at the manner in which the Sabbath day is observed here. Business is almost universally suspended, except by those of that denomination who observe the last day in the week, if any, and even they have but few customers. There is a universal relaxation from all the worldly cares of the week. The places of public worship are well attended, the streets are thronged with well-dressed people walking to inhale the fresh air after a week's toil, while those who have the means take an excursion to the Presidio or the Mission. The sounds of music and the rattling of dice are hushed for the nonce, and in the saloons, where on other days in the week throngs of young and old assemble to stake their substance at the gambling table, you see a quiet and peaceable set of men...Though the people have more leisure, there is less absolute intemperance and rioting on Sunday than other days. Even the exhorter on the piazza of the old adobe is attentively listened to by a large audience, and those who do not believe in that style of religious instruction, pass quietly on, paying proper respect to the opinions of others. The signs of licentiousness are less evident than common, and the heart is made glad by the sight of virtue in female garb, which can appear on that day without fear of coming in contact with flaunting and gaudily-dressed courtesans. For the most part, their loud and coarse laughter is hushed in the public thoroughfares and the moral atmosphere rendered purer. The evening too, is equally marked with quiet, and the streets present an animated appearance, alive with persons, but not dashing, pushing, and jostling their way through the streets, as if, when the sun went down, their lives were to be ended. *There is yet much room for improvement,* ***but we may still congratulate ourselves upon the observance of the Sabbath in San Francisco.***[37]

From these humble beginnings, Protestantism dates its birth on the Pacific slope, and its growth has more than kept pace with the increase of population.

FIRST CONGREGATIONAL CHURCH, COR. CALIFORNIA AND DUPONT STS.

Dedicated July 10th, 1853.

First Congregational Church, San Francisco, early 1850's.

San Francisco by 1878. "Sketches and Incidents of Travel on the Pacific Coast"
– a View of Montgomery Street. Courtesy of California State Library.

CHAPTER VIII

California – 1768-1848

For 80 years, prior to 1848, the **Disciples of St. Francis** had undisputed and undisturbed **possession of all California**. They were guarded by the soldiery, not of the King of Kings, but of the occupant of the throne of the Spanish monarchy. They had their heart's desire. They exercised regal sway and rolled in regal wealth. Of silver, of cattle, sheep and horses, they had unaccounted thousands. They built missions, dug irrigating ditches and dammed up the streams of water. They used the Indian converts to their religious faith in accomplishing all these; but to what end or purpose, aside from the mere gratification of human ambition? Nothing, absolutely nothing.[1]

1848 – California Missions in Decay

In 1848, the missions were in decay, the Indians were dead and in their happy hunting grounds, or strayed from the patristic roof. The friars had been despoiled of their gains, and many of them had sought other fields of labor. The shadows of the middle ages seemed to have reappeared, and settled, like a pall of night, over this whole coast.

There were, in **1848, no schools of learning, no newspapers, no books** outside of the meager libraries of Catholic missions, and no free, intelligent manhood.

The discovery of gold ended this medieval stagnation – this contented mental and moral stupor. The gathering nations overwhelmed the Spaniards and natives, and jostled each other in their struggle for gold; but at the beginning, as if **ordered in the councils of Omnipotence,** came the brave, the faithful and earnest **representatives of the Son of God,** and in His name demanded a place and a hearing among men who had forgotten all, for what never has and never can satisfy the yearnings of a single human being on the earth.[2]

The old **Placer Mines,** once filled with multiplied thousands of men of all lands, became deserted, except by the patient, **industrious Chinese**. The eager hosts have passed away. Their names have faded from the memories of men; but not so with the **Four Pioneer Founders** who arrived on the *"California,"* and those who came after them. Most of them "rest from their labors, but their works do follow them."

Amid tears and sorrow, poverty, deprivation and want, they did their work. They had **little of the gold of California** or of the wealth of this world. They **wanted little**. Below-cited are the results of these early Protestant efforts. They are recorded as monuments to the memory of men who, when the final results are summed up, will be found to have accomplished more for God and humanity, for time and eternity, than all the financial kings that ever lived in California.[3]

California – January, 1876

It will be seen that the Protestant Christian Churches comprised: *Methodist Episcopal Churches* – 97; Sabbath schools, 124; Scholars, 11,000; *Methodist Episcopal Churches South*: Ministers – 58; Sunday schools, 60; Teachers, 370; Scholars, 2,500. *Congregational Churches* – 63; Sabbath schools, 70; Scholars, 6,500. *Baptist Churches* – 80; Sunday schools, 70; Scholars, 5,000. *Presbyterian Churches* – 90; Ministers, 95; Scholars, 7,500. *Episcopalian Churches* – 40; One Bishop; Ministers, 36; Sunday school teachers, 400; Scholars, 4,000. *United Brethren Churches* – 20; Preachers, 10; Sunday schools, 6; Scholars, 300. *Christian Churches* – 50; Ministers, 55; Sunday schools, 50; Scholars, 2,500. *Cumberland Presbyterian Churches* – 40; Ministers, 40; Sunday schools, 25; Scholars, 1,500.[4]

California in Retrospect - 1847

Such are the results in twenty-six years. In **1847** there was not a **Protestant church** in California – never had been one. There was not a **public school** – there never had been one. There were no **newspapers** – nothing but the old Latin civilization, more than fifteen centuries old, engrafted on the ignorance of the native races of the Pacific Coast.

First Public School in California
built by Walter Colton - 1848

Walter Colton built the first public school house in California, in Monterey in 1848. He had brought with him the ways of the Puritan Fathers, and resolved that, so far as he could accomplish it, the church and public school should go together; and they have done so. It will be seen that there were, **in 1876,** in the Protestant churches named: *Churches,* 560; *Ministers,* 842; *Members,* 33,600; *Sunday schools,* 575; *Scholars,* 43,140; totaling 77,325. This represents a population of 500,000 souls, with an aggregate church property worth $2,290,000.[5]

Free Schools of California

Intimately and **inseparably connected** with these churches, ministers, Sunday schools and scholars, are the free schools of California, which are justly the pride of every intelligent, patriotic citizen. The school system of California was established as almost exactly that of Illinois, only the teachers were better paid.

Hence, it will be seen that *Anglo-Saxon Civilization* in **1876** had become firmly rooted and was in complete control all over California. No one denomination lorded it over another. All were equal before the laws, and all depended for success on their zeal for good morals, peace, charity and love. No *toleration* existed. There was absolute *religious freedom.*[6]

A Tribute to the Pioneer Founders
of California

Such is the tribute to the memory of **a few men** who **laid the foundations**, broad, deep and strong, of the religious, social and educational structure of the Pacific Coast, amid struggles for the metals never before witnessed by man, and which will, perhaps, never be repeated.

> The memory of the just is blessed
> but the name of the wicked shall rot.
> Proverbs 10:7

Old Poster on the Report of the Discovery of Gold sent to President Polk by Colonel Mason.

Scales used by Gold Dust Buyers.

CHAPTER IX

The Discovery of Gold
Coloma, California - 1848

"Monday 24th. This day some kind of mettle was found in the tail race that looks like goald, first discovered by Jan H.P. Martial, the Boss of the mill. Sunday 30 clean and has been all the last week our metal has been tride and proves to be goald. It is thought to be rich. We have pict up more than a hundred dollars worth last week."

(***The Journal of Henry Bigler***, established the date of the gold discovery in California.)

James W. Marshall –
Discoverer of Gold

"Boys, I believe I have found a gold mine," so said James W. Marshall to his mill workers on January 24, 1848, after he discovered gold in the tail race of **Captain John A. Sutter's** sawmill at Coloma. This discovery started the great gold rush to California, which preceded its admission to the Union as the 31st State on September 9, 1850. **Coloma** thus became the main supply and distribution cen-

Photograph of Sutter's Sawmill, Coloma, California.
Courtesy of California State Library.

ter for the miners working the hills and canyons in all directions. From it were founded other camps to the north, south, east and west. **Sutter's Sawmill**, owned by John Winters and Alden Bayley, ran day and night. Coloma boasted more board houses than any other town.

In July, 1848, Colonel Mason visited the mines and made an examination of the gold-bearing placers. His report to **President Polk**, who included it in his annual message to Congress, verified the gold discovery and resulted in quickening world-wide excitement. On December 7, 1848, Lieutenant Loeser arrived in Washington with a tea can containing 230 ounces, 15 pennyweight and 9 grains of gold, sent to President Polk by Colonel Mason.

The Gold Rush to California had begun.

Miners' Cabins

The earliest structures were canvas tents made from recycled cloth taken from abandoned ships in San Francisco Bay. **In 1849, Coloma** had hundreds of "tent" cabins. When the miners found they would be here for longer periods, they began building more permanent homes, such as log cabins.

Where Gold is Found

Gold is found is small quantities nearly everywhere in the earth's crust. Miners can only profit when they locate it in sufficient concentrations, typically in one of two types of deposits: a lode or a placer deposit. Lode deposits consist of veins of gold that have formed in cracks in the earth. Placer deposits consist of loose gold that has accumulated in valleys, often amid the sand and gravel of riverbeds like that of the American River. In some cases, prospectors who arrived early in the California Gold Rush literally filled their pockets with such gold-bearing rocks and nuggets.

Placer Mining at Coloma

When quartz decomposes, small pure gold particles are freed. They wash downstream and collect as placer gold in sand and gravel bars along Sierra rivers. Placer mining was the simple, but exhausting task of washing tons of sand gravel and dirt to recover ounces of gold. Miners found gold mainly in the American River's gravelling bed or in gravel terraces along its banks. Depending on the size of their operation, they washed dirt in pans, cradles, long toms, or sluice boxes. The heavy placer gold settled to the bottom of a pan or caught in the riffles of a sluice.

The Sapling Stamp

Miners easily made a primitive one-stamp mill from a young tree. With the help of the sapling's spring, they raised a crusher and pounded gold ore in an iron kettle or stone mortar. The crushed rock was then panned to remove the gold.

The Chile Mill

Many experienced gold-miners came to California from Chile in 1848 and 1849. They introduced the **Chilean Wheel**, which crushed ore beneath heavy, round stones. These mills were identical in design to mills used in Palestine during Biblical times for crushing olives, and were familiar to European gold-miners as early as the 16th century.

The California Stamp

Soon after miners discovered gold in underground quartz veins, mills were brought in to process ore. Dating back to at least the 1500's, the mills used heavy iron pounders called stamps to crush the rock. Each mill had a series of stamps

Panning for Placer Gold on the Stanislaus River. Harper's Magazine.

equipped with iron "shoes." Partially broken quartz was fed into bins behind the stamps and then into mortars holding dies on which the shoes fell. Each stamp rose and dropped separately. California quartz miners improved Stamp Mills by changing from soft iron to cast-iron shoes, dies and mortars. They also introduced stamps that rotated on the vertical axis with each rise and fall. The result was the "**California Stamp**," a machine so efficient it was used in gold mining throughout the world.

Using the "Long Tom" to sluice for Placer Gold. Harper's Magazine.

Hydraulic Mining

As miners moved from Sierra streams to gulches and hills, they found rich gold deposits in ancient river beds, some far from water. By 1853, they had begun working these gravels with water delivered through hoses and nozzles. Ultimately, this major California mining development created a vast system of flumes to satisfy its need for water. Brought from higher elevations in riveted pipes, the water was directed through iron nozzles called monitors. The powerful spray leveled hills and washed gold deposits into a series of sluices.

Hydraulicing also swept a large amount of silt and gravel into the Sacramento and San Joaquin Rivers, causing frequent flooding. Valley farmers organized, and in 1884 a court decision made hydraulic mining operators liable for downstream damage. Required to impound mining run-off, most companies found further hydraulicing unprofitable, and the industry virtually came to an end.

The Arrastra

Mexicans introduced the mule, or horse-powered arrastra to California in 1849. Gold-bearing ore was ground between heavy stones and a surface of well-fitted rocks. Miners then panned the pulverized ore to collect the gold. The arrastra was effective, but too slow for the impatient Americans.

The "Arrastra" – crushing gold-bearing quartz near Hornitos.
Harper's Magazine.

"A Miner's Reverie" – 1858

...I see around me, even in the rocks amidst which I toil
the relics of fleeting centuries...fossilized and preserved
for me to wander upon, study and meditate...But when I

A Chinese Miner panning for gold, 1872.
Courtesy of California State Library.

The Wah Hop Chinese store, Coloma, California.

look within myself as one for the whole, what do I find? A being full of varied instincts, endowed with reason and intelligence, capable of mighty deeds; but chiefly fritting away life's precious moments in endeavors to accomplish **unattainable things**, full of lofty aspirations, full of low and groveling pursuits, performing deeds in body and mind that would shame the face of day, and were they known unto men, would place many – O how infinitely too many! – upon the black rolls of infamy. Yet in me there is a ruling instinct high over all. It is an innate desire for immortality...but looking carefully throughout the universe, do I see the desire that is in us all, **the paramount wish for happiness and immortality?**

I see in the broad field of nature, marked upon every blade of grass, every leaf that trembles in the soft air of Spring, evidence that **there is a God**; there must be a Creator, an intelligence above our own.

There is in us a greater or less desire to know more than we can see in nature's field, about **this Supreme Being**. I have passed over the tomes of the past; made myself familiar with the views of the great men of former ages, their schemes of salvation and views of immortality; what they have said of the soul and its mysterious connections with the body, and I have searched profane history in vain for the plan of salvation that satisfied the full wants of the soul. **Man could not originate the plan, it was left for God Himself, and fulfilled in the person of Jesus of Nazareth.** No man ever lived that equaled him in beauty and symmetry of person, in godlike attributes and actions. Man cannot propose such a plan of salvation. **The Saviour's death was the most sublime scene ever recorded in history.** "Socrates died like a philosopher, but Jesus Christ, like a God."

My situation is that of many; the mountains are full of men, toiling for subsistence; they are found in every cañon, and on the hilltops. Many have given up in despair and turned drunkards, gamblers, loafers, villains and scapegraces. Others have gone down to untimely graves, beneath the weight of corroding cares; but I will maintain my own self-respect and endeavor to deserve the respect

View of Agua Fria Town. A mining town.
Courtesy of the Society of California Pioneers.

of others. I as firmly believe that industry, perseverance and energy will finally succeed, as that **there is a future life** of which **this is but the beginning;** these qualities are always equal to talents, and often superior; thousands of examples all over our country, lead me onward. "Excelsior" should be our motto under all circumstances.

No matter how lowly your situation or how dejected your thoughts, there is hope of success while there is life. The whole field of **nature was created by God himself**, and given you for a heritage. The earth, the air, the sun that illumines the heavens, the stars that gem the universe, all minister to your pleasure and happiness. And **Jesus the Son of God died for you upon Calvary**, that **eternal life** and happiness may be **yours.** That land beyond the grave you can inherit.[1]

Chinese Miners of the Mother Lode

Following the California Gold Rush of '49, swarms of **Chinese miners** came to make their mark on the diggings in the mother lode, including the **Coloma Valley.** They were *industrious and self-contained* and mostly content to thoroughly comb the old diggings. Thus, they reclaimed much gold that would have been overlooked. Chinese merchants came to serve their needs, such as **Wah Hop**, who ran one of the two stores still standing, known as the **Wah Hop** and **Man Lee** stores. The latter were built by Jonas Wilder before 1860 and leased to Chinese merchants. Located at the edge of a large **Chinese Community,** they sold traditional foods, clothing and other items. Such stores were also social centers and places for receiving news about other **Chinese Communities** in the State. After a disastrous fire destroyed **Coloma's Chinese Quarter** in 1883, most of the Chinese left town.

In journeying back to the days when Coloma was a tent city of thousands, each person intent on turning every bit of ground and gully that might yield the glint of gold, we find there were almost as many **different Protestant Christian** denominations as nationalities among the miners. But keeping **the Sabbath** was often forgotten in the frenzy to find the precious metal; most miners spending Saturday or Sunday preparing for the coming week.

Eventually, though, groups of men holding the same Christian faith banded together in the primitive little village of Coloma to share not only the labor of placer mining, but **Spiritual worship and prayer** as well.

Emmanuel Episcopal Church, circa 1855. Coloma, California.

Coloma's Early Days –
Eight Community-supported Churches

Among the links to California's history, is one of eight different churches supported by the community in Coloma's early days. **Emmanuel Episcopal Church** remains among three prominent houses of Christian worship in Coloma on Main Street. It was built in 1855, and is the oldest Episcopal church building in California. This lovely edifice is called a "carpenter's Gothic" because of the unique details of wood construction. *Rev. William Kip* began its work in Coloma. "Emmanuel" church, which means "God with us" was later acquired and used by the **Methodists.** This beautiful historic church was the site of James Marshall's funeral services in 1885.[2]

The Methodist Episcopal Church

Rev. William Roberts, superintendent of the **Oregon-California Mission**, went to Coloma in 1849 with **Rev. Elihu Anthony** and J.H. Dye, organizing the church and leaving Rev. Anthony in charge. In 1850, Rev. Isaac Owen, presiding elder of the California district, went to Coloma and put the new church on a firmer basis, appointing Rev. Warren Oliver as its pastor. It was the first of the Methodist Episcopal denominations in the Mother Lode, El Dorado County, taking second place only to the Baptists – but the first to build a structure unto Almighty God. Silas F. Bennett, who had been sent to Coloma from Sacramento by **General Sutter** to complete the mill, was the first **Bible Class leader** of the church in 1849.[3]

Circuit Preachers

Because of the transient atmosphere, pastors came and went, usually in a year's time. From 1862-1903, *Rev. C.C. Pierce* traveled the circuit, preaching to four different churches in four different cities: **El Dorado, Diamond Springs, Placerville and Coloma.**

"A Model Day for a Pilgrim"

He traveled with his carpet bag full of Sunday school papers and Bibles. On a beautiful day, Brother Pierce would be seen walking down the streets of Placerville, and if you stopped and asked him how he was, he would reply, "A model day for a pilgrim." If it was raining and you saw him out walking and offered him a ride, he'd reply, "Why should I ride when my Master walked?"[4]

College of California, circa 1868. Brayton Hall and College School.
Courtesy of California State Library.

CHAPTER X

The College of California
alias, The University of California, Berkeley

At the Golden Jubilee of the University of California in 1910, President Benjamin Ide Wheeler called **Rev. Samuel Hopkins Willey** "founder, prophet, seer, beholder," declaring in his citation: "Upon you, the foremost benefactor of California, first citizen of the State, I confer the degree of Doctor of Laws."

Today, the **University of California, Berkeley** has almost 31,000 undergraduate and graduate students. Its faculty includes 10 Nobel Prize winners and 82 members of the *National Academy of Sciences*. How did it all begin, however?

It has been this author's privilege to research and copy by hand, the hand-written personal *Notebook* of **Rev. Samuel Hopkins Willey**, an unpublished rare manuscript.[1] In it, Dr. Willey gives an intimate account of the **College of California**, of which he was a founder, stating that *"the transfer of the College of California to the State of California for the foundation of a University, was not accomplished in such a spirit and manner as might have been looked for, on the part of the authorities and representatives of the State."* Following is Dr. Willey's *Notebook* account:

Notebook of S.H. Willey

The following memoranda may be of use sometime. They will show that the transfer of the **College of California** to the State of California for the foundation of a University was not accomplished in such a spirit and manner as might have been looked for, on the part of the authorities and representatives of the State. But it is possible that the future history of the **University of California** may be such as to atone in some degree for the course pursued by the State authorities in the beginning, and make the Constitution a blessing to this State, the country and the world. 1888.

The closing paragraph of my *"History of the College of California,"* is as follows:

> After a delay of some months for the purpose of settling certain legal questions involved, the final transfer was made and all assets of the College were turned over to the University of California. The reason why these "legal questions" came up for settlement at this late day was, that during the pendency of the question of the transfer, no such questions were known to most of the members of

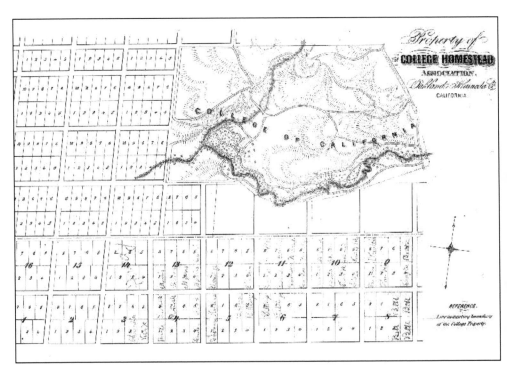

California, Berkeley (City) – Real Property.
"Property of the College Homestead Association" (186-)
Annotated to show land ownership.

the Board of Trustees of the College of California to exist. There were lawyers on that Board at the time, and they were depended on to guide the action of the Board in a safe way as to all matters of law.

No one of them suggested any doubt as to the legality of the proposition of the Board, on certain conditions, "to disincorporate and after discharging all its debts, pay over its net assets to such University."

Such a question was not so much as raised or spoken of. A sufficient reason why more attention was not given to the legal aspects of the proposed transfer, was that haste was necessary in coming to a conclusion.

It was already well on in the month of October, 1867, and the Legislature was to meet in the following December.

If the transfer was to be offered, **Governor Low** must know it soon, so as to recommend it in his message, and report in favor of it as Chairman of the *Agricultural, Mining and Mechanical Arts College Committee*, appointed by a previous Legislature to organize and locate that Institution.

There was not, therefore, sufficient time to deliberate concerning all the aspects of a transaction so important. Under the pressure of this necessity for haste to come to a conclusion, one way or the other, it was presumed that the way was legally clear, insomuch as no suggestions of doubt came from the law advisors in the Board.

The decision to make the offer of transfer was reached at the meeting of the Board held on October 8th, 1867. From that time all concerned in accomplishing the transfer had to work with the utmost diligence and even then they barely got their work done in time to secure action by the Legislature before the close of its session.

The proposed **Berkeley** site had to be surveyed and a map made of it. The site included portion of land belonging to several owners. The titles to these portions had to be searched and all imperfections set right.

The plan for the University organization had to be made and formulated into a bill for the Legislature, and then in pressing the work, every possible exertion had to be made to press the matter. The first suggestion I ever heard, that there were legal objections in the way of what we were doing, came from **Rev. Albert Williams** of San Francisco.

Samuel Hopkins Willey. Courtesy of California State Library.

First Seal of the University of California.
Motto: "Let There be Light"

Christian College

This suggestion he made in a letter to some member of the Legislature during the pendency of the University bill before that body. It caused some remark at the time, but inasmuch as the points made had never been raised by the lawyer members of our Board, no considerable attention was given to them. Nevertheless, **Mr. Williams'** queries had in them matters of more legal import that was then thought. But more of this hereafter.

On March 21, 1868, the University bill was finally passed and went to the Governor, who in due time signed it and it became law. This was only a very few days before the adjournment of the Legislature. By the law, the Senate had the right to appoint some of the Regents, and the rest were to be appointed by the Governor. But the Senate, being crowded with business, and the close of the session, and not being able to make the appointment of the Regents belonging to them, with due deliberation, left the work to the Governor.

Governor Haight was a prominent member of the *Calvary Presbyterian Church*, San Francisco. He was a graduate of *Yale College* and a lawyer of fair talent. But he never showed any friendliness to the **College of California.** He always declined to contribute anything to its funds, and never attended its commencements or its meetings of "*Pacific Coast Alumni.*"

But he was a gentleman of good associations, and well acquainted with the **College of California** and its work, and the unusual part it had taken in bringing the University into existence. And it was believed that he would honestly and fairly

The College of California as it appeared in 1865.
Oakland, between 12th and 14th Streets and Harrison and Franklin Streets.

act in the appointment of Regents and show a decent regard for the supporters of the **College of California** in the organization of the University.

Instead, however, of hastening to discharge his duty, as a man of his familiarity with men of experience in educational matters could have done, he consumed a month or two in his deliberations and then brought together a Board of Regents in which were found some men of literary attainment, some successful businessmen of various faiths, but who knew nothing whatsoever of College or University life or organization. But the notable fact about *Governor Haight's Board of Regents* was, that not one recognized friend or supporter of the **College of California** for any considerable length of time was found on it. The Rev. Horatio Stebbins was the only exception to this remark, and he had been on the College Board of Trustees but a few years.

The course taken by **Governor Haight** in this matter excited a good deal of comment at the time, and was not easily explained, but *his definite purpose* came incidentally to my knowledge only last summer in this way. About the month of June last (1888) I met Professor William Alexander, D.D. in the cars one day, and we happened to speak of the University, and I mentioned to him the fact that Governor Haight declined to give any of the characterizing and historic friends of the **College of California** any voice in the organization of the University. His reply was in substance as follows:

> I knew that was so, in this way. I had then (about the time of the appointment of the Regents) just come to California, and I had occasion to meet **Governor Haight** about the time he was making up the Board of University Regents. Among other things he said to me then, 'those gentlemen' (referring to the well-known supporters of the **College of California**) 'expected to have a good deal to say about the organizing of the University, *but I'll see that they don't!'*

That remark of his explains all. His conduct in the premises was plain enough, actions speak louder than words – but it was singular that after twenty years, the very words that expressed his purpose were repeated to me!

The Board of Regents spent the months of May and June in getting organized and in determining how to take up their work. Early in July, 1868, they addressed this communication to the **Trustees of the College of California**:

> At a meeting of the *Board of Regents of the University of California*, the following resolutions were adopted unanimously–
> **Resolved:** That the Regents of the University convey to the

Trustees of the **College of California** their high appreciation of the enlightened liberality evinced by that body in its proposal to donate its whole property to the University, and disincorporate on the organization of the *College of Letters* with its full course of studies. That regard for the highest interest of the University alone prevents the present acceptance of the offer; and it is therefore suggested to the Trustees of the College of California that their organization and classes be maintained another year, at the end of which time it is expected that the University will be so far organized and advanced that they can with better light determine whether or not to transfer their students to it and disincorporate.

Resolved: That the President of the Board of Regents be requested to transmit the above resolutions to the Trustees of the College of California. A true copy, Jms S. Gillan, Temporary Clerk.

This courteous and appreciative communication was accompanied with another from **Governor Haight**, President of the Regents, which reads thus:

College of California, circa 1868. Brayton Hall and College School.
Courtesy of California State Library.

Chapel. Brayton School, College of California, 1865.
Courtesy of California State Library.

San Francisco
July 3, 1868

To the Trustees of the
College of California

Gentlemen:

Enclosed are certain resolutions adopted by the Board of Regents of the University of California at a meeting held on July 2nd instant. The terms of the first and principal resolution leave me nothing to add except that I cordially concur in the appreciation which it expresses of the liberality and public spirit evinced by your Board in the donation of the present admirable site to the State University, and in the further offer to donate to the latter the entire property of your corporation. I trust the future history of the University will be such as to reflect lasting honor on the State, and upon all who have labored and sacrificed in the noble course of learning and education.

With much respect,
Your obedient servant,
H.H. Haight
President of the Board of Regents

In response to the request contained in the first of these preceding papers, and in due appreciation of the gracefully expressed sentiments of the other, a special committee was appointed to superintend the conducting of the College as requested, another year. But of the $15,000 or more, the Regents agreed to loan the College the sum of $10,000, and at a meeting of Trustees held August 25th, 1868, it was noted that a note be given for that sum. The note was given accordingly, the money was drawn and deposited and was used for the support of the College during the year. It became my duty as the executive officer of the College to carry out, as fast as possible, the resolution of the Trustees "to discharge all its debts, and prepare to pay over its net assets to the University, and after that to disincorporate."

This was not an easy task, or a work to be accomplished in a day, except at a ruinous sacrifice. This, I set myself to avoid, if possible. According to the final schedule of property presented to the Board of Trustees, and accepted as true and fairly estimated by them, that property was worth $50,000.

It consisted of two College blocks in **Oakland** and the buildings on them, and the unsold building lots in **Berkeley,** together with the very valuable hill land east of the college site, and the *water works* already in operation, and the extensive water rights and franchises, some of which were perfected, and others in negotiation. Surveys were in progress for bringing in *Wild Cat Creek* and pouring its waters into a *Natural Reservoir*, only needing a single small dam to hold it, to the extent of a considerable lake. This property was what was left to the College after having donated their choice University site, consisting of 160 acres of land.

But there was a considerable indebtedness to be paid first, and then the purpose was, to endow a *Memorial Professorship in the College of Letters* of the University, and the preference seemed to be the *Professorship of Moral and Intellectual Philosophy.* The object, there, was to sell this property as fast as it could be done to advantage, and at the same time finish, as fast as possible the waterworks in the bringing in and impounding the waters of *Wild Cat Creek.*

I went about both these branches of work with all diligence. The surveys were completed. The proceeding before the court in Contra Costa County were prosecuted to a successful conclusion as the records of that court now show. The object was to so far perfect the waterworks as to sell the whole, the *Strawberry Creek works*, and the *Wild Cat Creek works,* to the University, in order to realize the necessary sum *to found the proposed Professorship*, commemorative of the College in that Institution.

I was hard at work about that time with Hon. Sherman Day, it was late in October, 1868, in surveying and measuring the dam proposed back of the present residence of C.S.A. Palmer, Esq., and after my fatigue, took a severe cold. I was in a condition to be seriously affected by it. I had been all along disappointed in my hopes with regard to the College, and I may say, as to the organization of the University also. And still my duties in the premises were so pressing as to call me out in all weathers, regardless of every exposure.

I was therefore in a condition, both mentally and bodily, to be brought low by disease. I was first attacked with congestion of the lungs, with high fever and delirium, followed by typhoid fever, which reduced me to the very verge of life. From the time I was taken, for one full month I laid entirely unconscious, so that I have no knowledge or recollection whatever of anything that transpired. It was full four months before I was so far recovered as to be carried out of doors for a short ride in the sunlight and open air. I was emaciated to the last degree.

But recovery, when once it was fully commenced, was rapid, and by about the end of March, 1869, I was able to take up my work again. If I rightly remember, it was about this time that I met Professor Durant, probably it was our first interview after my sickness, and in conversation about College affairs, and what had taken place during my confinement, he said that **Mr. Felton** (J.B. Felton, **one the Regents**) made this remark to him, "We are going to let the College of California slide." We could neither of us understand what that language might mean.

We recalled the language and spirit of the communication from the Regents, of July preceding (1868), the last that we had received from them, and remembered that we were then fulfilling <u>as</u> <u>a</u> <u>favor</u>, their request that we should conduct the College through that year, "that," (as they expressed it) "at the end of that time it is expected that the University will be so far organized and advanced that they, (the College) can with better light determine whether or not to transfer their students to it and disincorporate."

The College year was but little more than half gone.

The College work was going on according to the understanding. There was no visible organization of the University. I am not sure whether the appointment of any Professors had been announced.

And what could be meant by the remark of Mr. Felton, **"We (the Regents) are going to let the College of California slide**," we would neither of us imagine. But we had not long to wait to find out.

A communication from the Board of Regents, dated April 6, 1869 explained all. It is printed in full in my history of the College. It consists of a series of resolutions, the first of which compliments the College for taking the action they did toward the creation of the University, reciting the resolutions of the College passed October 9th, 1867, and then in a subsequent resolution, the Regents say "we do hereby express to the Trustees of the College of California our readiness now to conclude the transactions by which their Institution and its effects are to be transferred to the University." This proposition was a complete surprise to the College Board, being

The College of California, circa 1868. Courtesy of California State Library.

so contrary to the spirit of that which next preceded from the Regents dated July 3rd, 1868. In that it was "suggested" to the Trustees of the College that the organization and classes be maintained another year, (now about half out) "at the end of which time it is expected that the University will be so far organized and advanced that they can, with better light, determine whether or not to transfer the students to it and disincorporate."

And now early in April, before the provisional year is much more than half out, and before any visible progress had been made toward the organization of the University and before there was any "better light" by which to "determine whether or not to transfer our students to the University and disincorporate," the polite and significant demand comes to us from the Regents to transfer everything to them at once to go out of existence!

That explained the meaning of Mr. Felton's significant remark, **"We are going to let the College of California slide!"**

For some reason, I know not what, **the Regents** seem to find themselves **in haste to see the College of California out of existence.**

The College surely, had no motive or desire to prolong its existence beyond the time necessary to dispose of its property, close up its affairs, pay its debts and embody, if possible, what might be left in the foundation of a Professorship, as heretofore indicated. But they were not pleased to be crowded out of existence, even politely, before any of these things were done.

And so, on the next day after the above-mentioned communication was received from the Regents, a committee was appointed by the College Board to confer with the Regents with reference to the matter and report to the Board at a special meeting to be held on April 16, 1869.

At the meeting held on the 16th, the Committee reported progress and asked instructions and further time. A free interchange of views then took place as to the powers of the Board of Trustees in the premises, when the following resolution was passed, viz. that the Committee of Conference be requested to take competent legal advice upon the question raised in their partial report, and report the conclusions in full at a meeting to be called by the secretary within ten days. It was further resolved that the Committee be requested to report at the same time their conclusions upon the general relations between the Board of Trustees and the Board of Regents, either as matters of law, or moral obligation.

At the next meeting of Trustees, held on April 26, 1869, the Committee of Conference reported progress again and recommended that the communication of the

University Regents of April 6, 1869 to this Board be answered, and that that Board be informed that the proposition made by them raised at once the question of the power of this Board in the premises, and that this Board is engaged in determining what that power is, as soon as possible, and that this must be settled as preliminary to the further consideration of the matters relating to the transfer of property to the University.

The Committee of Conference was also instructed to agree, on the part of this Board, upon a "case," by which should be submitted to the courts for their decision the questions of the power of the Board to "disincorporate and pay over its net assets to the University, after discharging its debts."

This action of the College Board was communicated to the Regents on the following day, April 27. The essential facts upon which the controversy depended were then drawn up in proper form, as appears by a copy in these archives. It recites the leading facts of the origin and history of the College, its incorporation, its sources of income, its Organic Basis and Rules, its acquisition of real estate, by purchase, its having made a donation of 160 acres of land to the State as a site for the University, its previous application (in 1854) to the College Society, East, for donations to its funds, its receipts therefrom, amounting in all to about $7,000.00.

Then was recited the action of the College Board offering to donate its site and property as the foundation of a State University, dated October 1867, and the action of the State, March 23rd, 1868, organizing the University.

Then the question was stated, can the College do these things as it has proposed?

The matter being one of doubt in the minds of some of those interested, the "case" is submitted to the courts. This statement of the case in question was unanimously agreed to by the College Trustees at a meeting held on May 25th 1869.

As the reasons for the doubt on the part of the College Board as to their power in the premises, a "brief" on the subject was prepared, and presented, and it is to be found in full in one of the books in the archives (note: It has been deposited with the memoranda herewith). This brief supported the proposition that the College Board had no power to disincorporate. To show this, it *first* recited the act of incorporation. *Second*, the vesting of the property in the Trustees for the use of the College. *Third*, the statutes defining the powers of the Trustees, and mentioned that "disincorporating" is not among them. *Fourth*, corporations are bound to follow strictly the letter of the Charter, and exercise no power unless granted. *Fifth*, the Legislature cannot meddle with College property or extinguish its corporate existence. *Sixth*, no authority in the government to control such a corporation or its funds. *Seventh*, a College Corporation is a private one, for perpetual distribution of the bounty of the founder. *Eighth,* the College Trustees have no power to give away the property. *Ninth,* it is a private College, as laid down by Chief Justice Marshall in the Dartmouth College case. *Tenth,* every founder of a College has a right to inquire into the administration of funds. *Eleventh.* Is this visitorial power a power to revoke the gift, to exchange its uses, etc.? No. It is a mere power to control and arrest abuses, and to enforce a due observance of the statutes of the charity. *Twelfth.* The statutes of the charity of the College provide that the Trustees shall have power to sell, mortgage, and otherwise use and dispose of such property in such manner as they shall deem most conducive to the prosperity of the College. It cannot give or donate the property of the College to any person or corporation. It cannot annihilate its powers and franchises. It cannot extinguish its corporate existence. *Thirteenth.* If lands are given to a corporate body and it is dissolved, they will revert to the owner. This "brief" as any one will see, on examination, is full and is supported in the margin by numerous references to legal authorities and decisions of courts.

But on consulting **John B. Felton, a Regent**, and presenting to him the statement of the case, as it had been unanimously adopted by the College Board, he stated most emphatically that he would not go before the courts to advocate the legality of the proposed action of the College Board in "disincorporating" and "paying over its net assets to the University," on that statement!

And yet, neither he, or any one else ever questioned the truth of that "statement" in a single particular!

Mr. Felton's declining to meet the case in court on that "statement" was an emphatic confession that the legality of the transfer and our "disincorporation" could not be sustained.

But Mr. Felton made the very singular proposition that the College Board should authorize him to employ "at his own expense" five of the leading lawyers of San Francisco to recommend to our Board a course by which our resolutions of October 8, 1867 could be carried into effect.

At a special meeting of our Board held June 9, 1869, it was voted that other proceedings being waived for the time, Mr. Felton's proposition be acceded to, it being understood that whatever recommendation might be made should be submitted to the decision of the Supreme Court. Nothing further, however, was heard of this proposition!

On the 12th June some friends of the College and University proposed the dividing of the question at issue and devising a way to settle the title to the 160 acres first, a thing desired by all parties, and leave the question of the power of the Board to disincorporate and give away property, to be judicially determined afterward.

This proposition was favorably received by all and was made definite by a letter signed by all the members of the College Board addressed to the Board of Regents. It stated the embarrassment that the College Board found itself in, and the earnest desire that a course might be taken to remove any cloud from the title to the University site donated to the State by the College Board.

And this it was proposed to do on the ground of the increase of value to the remaining land owned by the College in the vicinity consequent upon the location of the University on that site. That being so, there could be no violation of trust in the transaction. This would only leave to be determined the legal powers of our Board to disincorporate, and donate the remainder of its assets to the University.

At a Conference held between the Committee of the College Board and the Law Committee of Regents, it was agreed that, by a friendly suit between the parties, it should be sought to quiet the title to this 160 acres of land and for this only.

A statement of facts, as the basis of this suit was drawn up. It recited the facts in the same way as did the former statement, only confining itself to saying that the College Board offered, and the State accepted, the 160 acres site and that the college still retained about 200 acres of land in the vicinity which was greatly enhanced in price by the location of the University. It owns lands in Oakland also, that have increased largely in value, so that the value of its property now on hand is at least equal to the amount of donations ever made to the College.

This statement, which may be found in full in the Letter-book, before mentioned, was presented to the College Board by Hon. S.B. McKee, member of the Law Committee of Regents on July 14, 1869. The Board adjourned without acting on it on that day, in order to consult Hon. S.M. Wilson as to whether the case as submitted by this statement would involve any matter beyond the determination of the title of 160 acres of land.

On the following day, Mr. Wilson returned the "statement," giving as his opinion that the case thus presented would involve only the validity of the title to the 160 acres, and would not touch the question of the legality of disincorporating, or donating the balance of the property by our Board.

Under this advice, and on this understanding, the College Board on July 15, 1869 voted its agreement to the statement, and instructing Mr. Wilson to sign the same on behalf of our Board. He also was depended on to appear in the case and present it in our behalf.

The case was thus submitted to the Supreme Court about the middle of July, 1869. Mr. Felton, however, had it all his own way in behalf of the Regents. Mr. Wilson, according to my recollection, not appearing at all!

Instead of confirming the question according to the agreement, to the quieting of the University title to the 160 acre site, it took the wide range which Mr. Felton proposed to give it before the five lawyers whom he proposed to get to deliberate, "in what way we could legally disincorporate, donating all our property to the University!"

Paying no attention to the "agreement" in the premises, and having no counsel in our behalf to hold him to it and inform the court just what was submitted to them to decide, he presented the whole matter in his own way, arguing it wholly in the interest of the University, and without any opposing argument, and so it was submitted, substantially to the court, whether there was any possible way in which these gentlemen can give everything to the University and get out of existence as a College.

This latter question we had proposed to take up, subsequently, and see that it was properly argued, upon its merits. But here, when we were awaiting a decision according to agreement, on one point, one was procured that covered the whole ground, without our having the opportunity to say one word in argument in favor of our view of the law in the case. (The printed "decision" of the court is among the papers deposited herewith).

It was an immense surprise to the members of our Board. The text of this decision in full, as published at the time, may be found in the Letter-book heretofore referred to. Mr. Wilson was consulted as to his opinion of the bearing of the decision.

It was, that it quieted the title to the 160 acres of land that it leaves it to the option of the College Board whether or not to disincorporate, and that if this is done, the franchise must be surrendered, and the property given over to the State, and be also accepted by the State, to make the transaction valid. No sooner had this decision been announced, than the following brief note was received by the College Board:

San Francisco, August18, 1869

**To the President and Trustees
of the College of California**

Gentlemen:

The Supreme Court of California having decided that you may have power to surrender your franchise and transfer all your corporate property, after payment of your debts to the University, and thereby, the only obstacle having been removed which prevented your action, we beg to be informed whether your Board are prepared to carry out the proposition made October 8, 1867.

We are very respectfully yours,
S.F. Butterworth
W.C. Ralston
Executive Committee
Board of Regents

Without especial haste, the College Board replied as follows:

College of California
September 1, 1869

**To the Executive Committee of
Regents of University**

Gentlemen:

At a meeting of the **Board of Trustees of the College of California** held last evening, I was requested to reply to your letter of August 18, 1869 and say, that this board is ready to comply with the terms of its resolutions of October 8, 1867, so soon as it can be done in accordance with the terms of the recent decision of the Supreme Court of this State, which requires that the surrender of the Charter and property shall be to the State and must be accepted by the same. In making this surrender it has always been the intention of this Board, and still is, first of all, to pay off all its debts of every kind, legal and equitable, and after that to segregate the remaining funds and employ them for the endowment of a *memorial professorship* in the University's *College of Letters*, on such conditions as may seem to this Board just and wise.

I am, very respectfully yours,
S.H. Willey
Secretary of Trustees of
College of California

133

We had just closed the College year during which the Regents asked us to maintain our organization, and carry on the classes "the end of which time it was expected that the University would be so far organized and advanced that they (the College Board) can, with better light determine whether or not to transfer the students to it and disincorporate."

The contrast between the tenor and spirit of the Regents' communication of July 1868 and August 1869 is striking.

There was no visible advancement of the University to increase the "light," whether we should "transfer our students and disincorporate," and yet we were put under all possible pressure to abandon all, at once, and go out of existence as a corporation, and let the Regents take our property and manage everything. And yet when a special Committee of our Board appointed October 15, 1869 met a Committee of Regents and asked that the note given by our Board to them for $10,000.00 to help carry on the College for the year at the request of the Regents, be remitted, as it had been expended in their service rather than in ours, the proposition was declined, and payment of the note on maturity by our Board was insisted on! (see the Report of the Special Committee in full in the Letter-book).

This condition of the relations between the College Board and the Regents reduced interest in the settlement of the affairs of the College to a low point.

It ought to be stated that none of the donors to the funds of the College objected to the transfer to the University except the representatives of the College Society at the East.

The Committee of that Society consisting of Rev. Dr. Leonard Bacon, Rev. Dr. Theron Baldwin and Norman White, Esq., wrote a letter which was received in August, 1869, inquiring into the facts and claiming that funds procured through the agency of that Society be returned us. But the claim was not pressed, the entire sum received from that source in 16 years being but about $7,000.00.

But it was noticeable that in the last **"statement of the case"** on which **Mr. Felton _went before the Supreme Court_** and got the decision, this particular donation was omitted. I do not know why, unless it was the particular one, on the ground of which any further question would be likely to be raised.

A full account of the whole matter was sent to Dr. Bacon and the Committee of the College Society. No further action was taken by the Society in the case, but the occurrence was made the occasion of adopting a new rule by them, to prevent future loss in a similar way.

It was now getting into the Fall of 1869. The first University class had been admitted, and instruction was commenced in our College buildings in Oakland under the three University professors who had been at that time appointed.

The College Board proceeded to close up its affairs as fast as possible. But with all the details of the business of the College work (i.e. the settling up of College business) on hand, especially that of the Homestead Company, and the Water Company, with property to dispose of (and debts to pay, and *with no disposition to help on the part of the Regents*), it was *an unpleasant and not a very hopeful undertaking*.

The Real Estate market, that Fall, was unusually dull, and no property could be sold, except at a sacrifice. The last communication to the Regents that I find among my College papers is one answering an inquiry about our Mountain Land. I copy it here in full because it shows that the Regents were informed of its extent, its title, and its importance to the use of the College site which we had donated to the State.

This is important, because of the subsequent disposition of this property by the Regents, and the litigation it involved them in through a series of years as to water, in which suit, at last they did not win.

San Francisco, December 30, 1869

S.F. Butterworth, Esq.
Chairman, Executive Committee of Regents

Dear Sir:

As suggested by you, we enclose a statement relative to the character and value of the hill land offered for sale by the **College of California** to the University and the price for which the College is willing to sell.

It consists of 108.56 acres lying east of the 160 acres heretofore donated by the college for the site of the **University of California** and is embraced in Plots nos. 80 and 82 of Kellesburger's map, and 112 acres adjourning the same, being a part of what is known as the undivided Mountain Land; in all 220.56 acres of land.

The 112 acres, although not legally divided and set off to the College, is fenced and in possession, and has been for 10 or 12 years, and is so situated that it can be of no considerable value to any but the owners of the present University property.

To this property this 220 acres seems to be almost a necessary adjunct. **It is a part of the water-shed of 800 acres** which supplies the water of the stream

(Strawberry Creek) running through the University grounds. It contains the Springs, also, which flow into the same stream. It contains a basin of some 8 or 10 acres where the stream leaves the hill land and flows down on the University site, at an elevation of from 100 to 150 feet above the location of the University buildings, where by the construction of a dam, only about 100 feet long by 60 feet high, over 13 millions of gallons of water can be impounded. An accurate survey of this basin was made by Hon. Sherman Day in October, 1868, together with the examination of banks and bottom for dam and drawings and estimates for dam, pipes, etc.

At least one third of this land is susceptible of cultivation, and being elevated and generally free from frost, offers facilities for many kinds of experimental cultivation that could not be also well made on the lands below. Had the College proposed to sell the water which they have given to the University, this land, with its water-shed, springs, and rare location, would have been invaluable for the water itself; could not have been controlled and used without it. In donating this water, and the water-works to the University, they have given what cost them nearly $20,000.00. The lowest price which we think the College ought to receive for this land is as follows:

For the 108.56 acres in plots nos. 80 and 82 of the Kellesburger's Survey, $175.00 an acre. For the 112 acres of the undivided Mountain Land, $25.00 an acre. And as authorized by the Board of College Trustees, we hereby offer to sell at these prices.

As throwing light on the question of the price, it may be proper to state that the land is assessed for taxes this year as follows:

The portion lying in plot No. 80 - $55.00 an acre. That in plot 82, $60.00 an acre, and the 112 acres of undivided land, $5.00 an acre. While no land in the valley below is worth less than $1,000.00 an acre, we think that no one can consider the price named above for the land in question, too high.

(signed)
S.H. Willey
Ira P. Rankin
Henry Durant

This report of remaining Berkeley property, owned by the College in December, 1869 I enclosed, February 27, 1889, to Hon. Horace Davis, President of the University, accompanying it with the following letter of explanation:

Congregational Church,
Benicia, California
27th February, 1889

Hon. Horace Davis

Dear Sir:

I found, a few days ago, the accompanying paper, which was mislaid and long forgotten. It is a report made by a **Committee of the Trustees of the College of California** to the Executive Committee of the Board of Regents of the University of California at the request of S.F. Butterworth, Chairman of the latter, **describing the Berkeley property remaining to the College of California** after donating the University site. It may have some historical value.

If you think proper, it may be placed with a few other similar papers which I have heretofore given, and which are in care of the Librarian. I have been often asked for papers of this kind, but in most cases I have to reply, that they went with those that I turned over to the Regents near the close of the year 1869.

Such, for instance, as the "Notes" of Mr. Day's surveys as to water, etc. and the *very costly set of maps, topographical drawings*, specifications of building sites, road-ways, plantings, etc., etc…made for the college by Fred Law Olmstead, Esq.

I am very truly yours,
S.H. Willey

To this note I received at once a very courteous reply, accepting the papers and saying they would be deposited as suggested in the Library. The real fact was, that **the property of the College**, after donating the site to the University, was worth at least **$50,000.00** – on which was an indebtedness of about $20,000.00.

Very soon after my communication of December 30, 1869 to the Regents, I re-signed my office as **Vice President of the College of California** and also as Secretary of the Board of Trustees.

It had become evident that the Regents did not wish to have the College close up its affairs and with its remaining property found and endow a professorship in the University. And unless this could be done, to save something of the influence of the College in the Institution it had brought into being, there was no sufficient motive for my giving further time to the service of the College. Besides, my health and strength were only partially restored from my long sickness, and every one said

I needed to get away from these depressing business affairs, and have an entire change of scene.

(**Note on opposite page**: Today, March 31, 1905, in the interest of a gentleman who is enquiring as to the title to certain property in Berkeley, I got liberty to examine the Records of the Regents for the years 1868-1870. It appears that though no adequate action was had as to water-supply, a special Committee was appointed to examine and report on the matter on November 24, 1868, consisting of Jno. B. Felton, Saml B. McKee and Edward Tompkins. I found no action recorded concerning the matter afterward. The **College of California** had signified to the Regents that it was their wish, after disposing of their property remaining, and paying all their debts, to use such funds as they might have in founding a ***"Memorial Professorship,"*** in the **College of Letters in the University**. In reply to this, Mr. Tompkins introduced a resolution that the Regents would <u>not</u> <u>permit</u> the closing up of the affairs of the College of California <u>with</u> <u>the</u> <u>University</u> <u>in</u> <u>this</u> <u>way</u>! A record dated March 2nd, 1869 states that the board of Regents "resolved <u>not</u> to ask the State <u>to</u> <u>change</u> <u>the</u> <u>location</u> of the University – and this resolution was passed 13 yea. 1 no. Mr. Doyle. Another point. – In the Regents' Manual it is stated that the <u>indebtedness</u> of the College of California was $5,405.00. That could only be made out by ignoring the fact that $10,000 used in 1869 in carrying on the College during its last year, at the <u>special</u> <u>request</u> of the Regents be charged against the College property – and, furthermore that the value of the <u>water-property</u>, which was more than $20,000 be left out of the assets of the College).

My resignation was accepted, and early in 1870, I went East, and remained almost the whole year. I never knew how matters were settled, further than that the College property and indebtedness were turned over to the Regents and there our affairs ended.

It afterward appeared that they sold the hill land, and with it went all the water sources of ***Strawberry Creek***, and the opportunity of improving water. No attention was paid to the preservation of the **College Water Company,** or of the legal rights that had been acquired under it. All were forfeited by neglect.

And, years after, when water sources had become very valuable, and had been taken up by private parties, and the University was almost without water, **the Regents tried by** long and expensive **litigation to recover something of that which had been lost; but they failed.** 1888.

Notes: "Relative to the action of the **Trustees of the College of California** in **fixing the permanent site** at the place afterward named **Berkeley.***

The inquiry for the best site was had in mind by the members of the Board from the early years. It was conducted very thoroughly during the year 1856 with the exceedingly valuable assistance of **Rev. Dr. Bushnell**. No conclusion was arrived at, however, during that year. Dr. Bushnell returned East early in January 1857, but the inquiry was prosecuted still with more or less vigor by the Trustees. The various places in San Mateo County, Santa Clara County, Alameda County, Contra Costa County, Napa County and Sonoma County reported on by Dr. Bushnell were reviewed and considered, and no one of them seemed to meet all the needful conditions.

The standing Committee of the Board touching a permanent site, consisted of Willey and Rankin. This Committee included in their report to the Board, a site not included in Dr. Bushnell's Report. It was described as about **four miles North East of Oakland on the Paralta Ranch,** near the residence of Captain Simmons.

The place presented many strong points for which we had been looking to find them combined in one spot, but it lacked a sufficient flow of running water. Nevertheless, the inquiry was commenced to ascertain whether a sufficient amount of land suitably located, could be obtained. It was carried on through the summer and fall of 1857, and resulted in ascertaining that the land needed could be obtained. The Report described the site in detail, and commended it to the attention of the Board. The Report presented February 23, 1858, was accepted and taken under consideration and the Committee was discharged.

After further consideration for several months, a meeting of the Board was called to take final action on the question of the **permanent location of the College**. It was held in San Francisco on March 1st, 1858. There were present Rev. Benton, Rev. Wadsworth, Mr. Rankin, Bishop Kip; Mr. Waller; Mr. McLean; Rev. Brierly; Mr. Page; Rev. Willey. The report of the Committee recommending the **Berkeley** site was taken up, and it was adopted by a unanimous vote of the Board.

Two years later, before taking possession of the property, it was deemed fitting by the Trustees that **the site should be formally and publicly set apart and consecrated to the purposes of education forever.**

---

* The name "Berkeley" was chosen by the Trustees of the College of California in honor of George Berkeley, Bishop of Cloyne, author of: *Westward the course of Empire takes its way.*

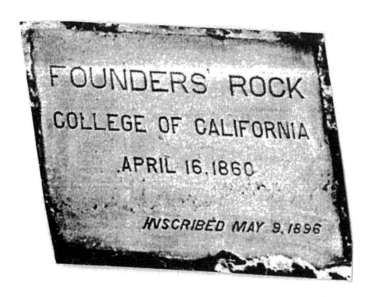

Founders' Rock plaque: "Founders' Rock – College of California – April 16, 1860."

Accordingly, a meeting of Trustees was called to be held on these grounds on **April 16, 1860.**

On the appointed day, we met on this, our chosen site, and spent the time in examining the entire locality, with references to the changing of it from a great grainfield, to be **the home of a College.** It was a delightful Spring day, and we fully enjoyed it. Before leaving, we looked about for some permanent landmark around which we could gather for some **simple ceremonies of dedication.**

What is now known as **"Founders' Rock"** appeared to be the only thing that met the requirements of the occasion, and so we made our way to it.

At that time, **standing on that Rock** commanded a view of the entire property we were examining. There were then no Eucalyptus trees, as there are now in great numbers, obstructing the view altogether. From this elevated spot, the grounds were all before us, covered with a crop of growing grain, and bordered with the noble old oaks and other trees as are now standing, and are considered of such priceless value.

Here **at this Rock**, the Board organized for business. There were present, Rev. W.G. Anderson, President; Rev. S.H. Willey, Secretary; Rev. E.S. Lacy; Rev. Henry Durant; Frederick Billings, Esq.; Rev. E.B. Goddard; Mr. Edward McLean and Ira P. Rankin, Esq.

The purpose of the meeting was fittingly stated by the President.

Thereupon, **a resolution was presented formally setting apart these grounds as the future and permanent location of the College of California.**

Upon this resolution, somewhat extended remarks were made by most of the members of the Board, particularly by the President, by Mr. Billings and by Rev. Mr. Durant. Then by unanimous vote, the resolution was passed. Thereupon, **the President, standing upon the Rock, surrounded by the members of the Board,** *with heads uncovered,* **offered prayer to God, asking His blessing** *in what we had now done,* **imploring His favor upon the College** *which we proposed to build here, and asking that the grounds might ever be* **the home of Christian learning and a blessing to the youth of this State** *and a center of the highest usefulness in all this part of the world.*

Then we adjourned, and returned some to Oakland and some to San Francisco.

(End of Rev. Samuel Hopkins Willey's handwritten **Notebook** account of the College of California, Berkeley).

College of California site, dedicated with prayer on April 16, 1860. "Founder's Rock," Berkeley.

CHAPTER XI

The College of California, Berkeley
Vice Regents' Report – July, 1869

Further to the foregoing, heretofore unpublished original account of the **College of California, Berkeley's** hidden past and its "disincorporation," the Vice Regent's Report – July, 1869, hand-written by S.H. Willey, throws more light on the subject:[1]

Vice Regent's Report
– July, 1869

It is desirable in this year's report, to take a brief survey of the past history and present condition of **the College**.

The preparatory department or **College School**, as it is called, was commenced in 1853. It was slowly built up to a self-sustaining point, and besides instructing hundreds in the ordinary branches of useful knowledge, it brought forward students ready to enter upon college standing in 1860.

Since that date, although this Board thought best to part with the proprietorship, the Institution has always been recognized by its owner, and by the public, as still a Department of the Collage.

It has been itself as truly a College all this time, as the other institutions in this State, known as Colleges have been, with only this difference, that in individual cases, some of them have advanced some students through the college course, to graduation.

The **College of California** alone has gone beyond this, and maintained the regular college organization of the four annual classes taught separately by a faculty exclusively employed in their instruction. This organization was established by this board in August 1860, and has been maintained to this time. The faculty consists of its executive officer and the Vice President, three professors, two of whom have been employed in the College exclusively, and three Instructors, one of whom has been wholly employed in the College and the other two, a portion of the time.

Six classes have completed their course of education in the College, and have graduated with the appropriate degree. **Three of the young men have already entered the ministry of the Gospel,** seven have commenced the **practice of Law**, **one** has become a **physician, one** a **mining engineer**. Others, more recently graduated, are prosecuting their professional studies. A bold stand has been made thus, early in the history of the State, in favor of liberal education. In our American system of education the college has its place. It does not propose to fit young men directly for business or professional life. This is the work of High schools and Seminaries, or of scientific and professional schools. But the College **undertakes to train men, as men**. It undertakes to do for the mind what the gymnasium does for the body. *It seeks to develop and strengthen the mental faculties by exercise, by a systematic and prolonged training*.

There are those among our youth who seek such culture. They take delight in this inspiring mental exercise. And they grow by means of it into a symmetrical and well-rounded manhood.

The number who seek this training here is small, as yet. The whole spirit of society is for the practical, the material, for enterprise, money making and using money.

But those who do seek this liberal education, ought not to seek it in vain. Young men of capacity ought to be encouraged to undertake it. They should be persuaded to take time for it while they are young, and before they come to the age when they should enter upon professions or prepare for business.

Then, when they do come into their professions, or assume the responsibilities of business life, it is with an ample and generous preparation. They come to their life-work trained to perceive, to reason, to discriminate, to judge and to express themselves in writing and in speech. With this preparation, they are able to excel, and they do excel.

The **College of California** has declared for this education, strictly so-called. This has been its standard. It may have been set up too early. The expensive work may have been undertaken a few years too soon. But it has been maintained firmly, for nine years, and it is not likely that it will be let down now.

We must have the University, with its department of Agriculture, of Mining and Mechanics, and of Law and Medicine, if you please, but it must contain a "College" properly so-called, with its standard well up, or it will not meet the expectations of the State in the long run.

In its nine years' work, the **College of California** has rallied many supporters around it. In this *it has done a great deal more than any other institution on this coast*. And when we compare it with the **beginnings of Colleges** in other new States, *I cannot find the statistics of one that has grown faster, or occupied more property in its first ten years*.

It has become known, and honorably known, more widely, perhaps than some of us think. Large numbers of the *Alumni of American and European Colleges and Universities*, resident in this State, have assembled at our Commencements, and in many ways have manifested sympathy with the College.

This has not only been of great service to the College, but it has organized a public sentiment in the State, among educated men, and created here a commonwealth of letters. This working together of the Alumni in this State, was eloquently alluded to by President Hopkins, in his late sermon before the *Western College Society*, as illustrating the sympathy of educated men with each other, and their *"readiness to work together in everything that will enlighten and elevate the community."*

The published addresses and proceedings of these literary festivals of ours have awakened a lively interest abroad, in many quarters, and they constitute no unimportant part of the best home-literature of the State.

The **College has derived its funds in the first instance from direct contributions.** These have been solicited from time to time, ever since the establishment of the *Preparatory Department*. This was done in all the early years by the voluntary efforts of numbers of this Board, sixteen years ago. They have been obtained in small sums. From the books, it appears that the whole number of subscriptions collected, is 431, and the total amount, is $58,825.77.

The largest of these donations, and the only one above $1,000.00 was that of the *Pacific Mail Steamship Company*, which was $5,000.00. Donations varying from $500 to $1,000 each – 8. In sums from $100 to $500 – 53. In just $100 sums – 231. In sums less than $100 – 138.

This analysis indicates **the amount of work it has cost to obtain so many subscriptions** and collect so many small sums. Besides, it must be remembered, that to obtain these **400 subscriptions**, it required applying to 3 or 4 times that number of individuals, for not more than one person in four subscribed, who was asked. But all the numerous conversations connected with these donations have contributed to make the College known, and make people feel some responsibility for sustaining it.

The analysis of these contributions, as respects the places from whence they came, further shows, as follows:

(Subsequently found in the books a donation of Rev. Henry Durant's, their principal at the College School in services, $1,290 which, if credited to Oakland, would raise its gifts to $2,498.12).

Oakland, where the college is located, has given $1,209. – San Francisco, $47,147. Sacramento, $4,450. Marysville, $1,443. Stockton, $400 – and from miscellaneous sources have some $2,177.77.

To this add, say $7,000 received at various times from the **Western College Society,** and it makes the total amount of cash contributions to the College in sixteen years since the commencement of the *Preparatory Department*, $63,825.77.

Within the nine years since the organization of the College proper, there have been paid out for salaries of Professors and Instructors, furniture, apparatus, books, printing, repairs and insurance $93,077.78 which sum is more by $29,522.49 than the entire amount of the cash contributions to the College.

This latter sum of $29,522.49 together with say $50,000 the present estimate net assets of the College, is what has been made on the Real Estate of the Institution (except a few thousand dollars received for tuition), besides providing the State University with its site, consisting of 160 acres of our most valuable land.

It thus appears that after paying all the expenses of the College for nine years, and furnishing the above-named site to the University, the Institution has left property, very nearly, if not quite, equal in value, to all the cash contributions ever made to it.

In accordance with the propositions heretofore made by the Board, **the use of our College building in Oakland has been offered to the State University,** for the time being, and in case that institution organizes its **College of Letters, we have proposed to relinquish our College classes to its care.** (If this arrangement goes into effect, the expenses of the College will come down for the time being to the mere cost of managing its property).

The important question pending, as the Board knows, is, whether we can "disincorporate," and after liquidating our debts, **"donate our net assets to the University"** according to our proposition of October 8, 1867.

There ought to be no unnecessary delay in reaching a proper determination of this grave question.

Till this is obtained, we cannot move to the right-hand, nor the left. It seems to become this Board to determine upon and adopt some method which it will accept, as a satisfactory settlement of the legal question pending. Then we can proceed, but not before.

If it should appear that **we can disincorporate** and donate our net assets; then will come the question <u>when</u> we will do it – <u>on</u> <u>what</u> <u>conditions</u>, or <u>specifications</u> we will do it, and in what form.

If, on the contrary, it should appear that we cannot legally disincorporate, then will come up all the questions of a continued and perpetual corporate existence, for the ends and purposes originally had in view.

If we cannot take the former course, and hand over our trust to the Regents of the University; we are bound to take the latter, and discharge the trust ourselves by providing our constitution (of some grade) **according to our pledge** heretofore publicly given, that will "**furnish the means of a thorough and comprehensive education, under the pervading influence and spirit of Christianity.**"

This certainly, we owe to ourselves, as charged with a trust for society, we owe it also to those who have furnished the means now in our hands, the living and the dead; we owe it to society here and elsewhere, which has had no small expectations of us; and we owe it to the coming generations who will one day review what we do now; and finally, **we owe it to Him, above all, to whose honor we have sought to consecrate all our work from the beginning**.

S.H. Willey
Vice President, College

On September 1, 1869, **Rev. S.H. Willey** responded to a letter of enquiry addressed to him by the *Committee of the Western College Society*, stating his "determination to transmit a full statement of all matters pertaining to the College of California and the University." Dr. Willey's hand-written letter – an intimate sketch of the **College of California's** "disincorporation," is cited in its entirety:

Copy of a letter to Dr. Theron Baldwin in reply to letter of inquiry addressed to S.H. Willey by Rev. Dr. Bacon, Norman White, and Rev. Dr. Theron Baldwin, Committee of the Western College Society.[2]

Rev. Dr. Baldwin

Dear Sir:

On the receipt of the letter of inquiry from the *College Society's Committee*, I addressed you a note, to the effect that no transfer of our College to the University had yet taken place, nor did it seem likely that it would take place, intimating also that I might see you early in the Fall, and give a full account of these matters. Since then, the aspect of affairs is so changed that I have determined to transmit to you a full statement of all matters pertaining to the College and the University, narrated in chronological order, consisting mainly of published pamphlets and documents on record, and thus submit the case to the judgment of your Committee, the Society and whomsoever else it may concern.

It goes by mail with this. On page five are stated the financial reasons why the Trustees of the College entertained the idea of getting up the University at the first.

Rev. Mr. Lacy had gone from the *First Congregational Church* in this city, broken in health; **Rev. Dr. Anderson** had gone from the *First Presbyterian Church* for a similar reason. **F. Billings, Esq.**, an early and liberal contributor and an able one, had gone for reasons also pertaining to health. **Rev. Goddard**, *another noble founder*, was dead. The men who had come to fill these men's places in California and in our Board, turned the scale in favor of prospecting a University and ultimately merging the College in it.

On pages 13 and 15 you will see the **Resolutions "of October 8, 1867."**

The reason they were passed in such haste was, that the State Commissioners were close upon the end of the term of office and must act then, or not at all. They (i.e. the Resolutions) were so unreserved, because *it was thoroughly understood that the College should be the germ, in its spirit and organization,* and the University the outgrowth. Even then the old friends and all of us main workers in the College held back to the last. But when the thing was done, we thought we would try and save **the spirit of the College,** in the University, if we could.

Two months later, however, in November, 1867, the Republican Party, strong and all through the War in power, split, disastrously between two candidates, and let in the Democratic candidates! The new officers were strangers to all these antecedents, understandings and pledges, and were far from being the men that even our Board would have trusted, had they known or suspected beforehand, that they would be in office.

Still, when the new officers came to understand the situation, they entered at first into full sympathy with it, and enacted a pretty good law (see page 18) and gave at once $200,000 to start with.

On page 24 of the University pamphlet it is stated how the Regents were appointed. This Law was finally passed only three or four days before the Legislature adjourned. The <u>Senate</u> not having time to appoint the first eight Regents with any deliberation, left it to the <u>Governor</u>, as per page 25, Sec. 61 of the University Law. Now **Governor Haight**, although a Democrat, is a professed Christian, a leading member of Dr. Wadsworth's O.S. Presbyterian Church – a graduate of Yale College, and a gentleman of good associations, well acquainted with our College, and what it had done toward the University. *It was believed he would act honestly and fairly. Just there was the failure.* Instead of sitting down as he could have done, and in a single week, appointing proper men, he consumed a month or two, and his eight appointments turned out to include Roman Catholics and indifferents or skeptics – **but no minister of the Gospel** (but one Unitarian) and **not one of the characterizing and efficient friends of the College**, *which had given the University its existence*, and without which as all will say, it could never have had an existence.

Small hopes of the University did the discerning friends of **the College and Christian Education** have from that day. The remainder of the Board was filled with men of the same type, and is two-thirds or three-quarters Democratic, and that of the ultra southern stripe. Hence the election of the General McLellan last Fall for President. We did not come, however, and no one fills that place yet. The two gentlemen first elected to the faculty were the Le Conts from South Carolina. Since that some northern men are appointed, among whom is Professor Kellogg of our College – the only appointment from among us.

Without having any more than begun to fulfill the conditions on which in our **Resolutions of October 8, 1867** we proposed to disincorporate and pay over the balance of our assets, the Regents sent us the communication found on page 21.

It was unexpected and astonishing. Then was appointed the Committee to look into the legal questions involved in the matter, of which I was made Chairman. Our reports, commencing on page 26, show the work we have done. For one, *I was early convinced that the whole proceeding was both legally and morally wrong,* and the documents show how utterly *the apposite party refused to try the case fairly on its merits*. For doing my duty as Chairman of this committee, **I was subjected to threats and various methods of pressure to drive me from my post.**

Various friends of Education suggested a division of the question, which resulted in the latter on page 54. On the basis of that was the statement for an "Agreed Case," page 57. If a decision on that could have been true and fair we could have sold our remaining property at an enhanced value and gone close to one of our largest cities, the capital, where our property could have been matched by as much more given there, where there is no institution, and so in a few years been better off then ever.

But, no, we must be put out of the way. So the statement for the "Agreed Case" was made to omit your donation entirely (see page 73) and then travels over ground never suggested in the "statement," and contrary to the repeated pledges of the parties, and as an argument covers the <u>whole</u> case, when only <u>one part</u> was agreed, or thought to be submitted under that <u>partial</u> <u>statement</u> <u>of facts</u>. The full statement of facts is found on page 42.

All this is reviewed in our final report on page 75. I have given my last **Executive Report** on page 112, to indicate our financial history and condition.

And so I submit the case to you, to all interested, and to the calm decisions of coming time. **I took up this work seven years ago, as a Christian minister**, on the urgent solicitation of the Trustees, and pressed with special persuasion by **Rev. Dr. Anderson, Rev. Lacy, Rev. Brayton, Rev. Benton, and others.** Nothing seems to remain, but to pay the debts, convert the property into money and found one or two such professorships as we choose, coupled with such conditions as are proper. See provisions of University Law, page 31, Sec. 73.

What you, as a Society, will say to this decision and these proceedings, I cannot tell, but the facts are before you. You must be the judges.

I have striven against this result with all my might, but it has been in vain. My family are now in Philadelphia. I am trying to get off overland to join them September 15th, but whether this business will let me off, I cannot say. If I go, I may see you. If not, **these documents must tell the story**.

I am very truly yours,
S.H. Willey

This author has allowed Rev. Dr. Samuel Hopkins Willey, honored as "founder, prophet, seer, beholder, foremost founder of California, first citizen of the State," to relate the true story of the *Christian* College of California being *"put out of the way" and taken over by the State authorities for their own purposes of secularism* – devoid of the College's firm adherence to Christian education.

To these **Pioneer Founders** belong honor and admiration, for their noble endeavors to educate the youth of California with enduring principles of Christianity, by founding and establishing the **College of California**: "Where the Spirit of the Lord is, there is Liberty."

2 Corinthians 3:17

Seal and Motto of the University of California –
*"Let there be light"**

*The Rail Splitter: This poster from Abraham Lincoln's 1860
presidential campaign showed forth his frontier origins.
Courtesy of Chicago History Museum.*

Chapter XII

America's First Transcontinental Railroad
A Path Through the Mountains

Railroad engineers and surveyors battled wilderness, weather and terrain to locate a route for the nation's first Transcontinental Railroad. Unlike road vehicles, trains require broad curves and a relatively level route. Finding such a path through the Sierra Nevada was the greatest single challenge the **Transcontinental Railroad** project faced. Using a variety of reconnaissance techniques, painstaking measurements and mathematics, **Central Pacific** survey parties found a suitable path through the mountains. The route required many expensive tunnels, bridges, cuts and fills. But the route did not exceed the maximum allowable grade of roughly two feet change in elevation for each hundred feet the track moved ahead.

Today, the original Central Pacific route is still a primary link between **California** and the nation. While it has been greatly improved, it remains a marvel of 19th century technology and a testament to the skill and perseverance of the surveying crews.

Surveying a Railroad route was difficult and often dangerous work. The **Central Pacific** and the **Union Pacific** routes of the Transcontinental Railroad both met with natural obstacles over the entire length.

The completion of the Transcontinental Railroad linked the nation's East and West halves, uniting America like no single event before or since.

President Abraham Lincoln signs
Pacific Railway Act –1862

The signing of the Pacific Railway Act by President A. Lincoln in 1862 marked the end of decades of planning, discussion and heated argument. Backed by considerable governmental support, construction of a transcontinental railroad began. The **Central Pacific Railroad** faced the formidable task of **crossing the Sierra Nevada Mountains**, as it began building east from Sacramento. The Union Pacific Railroad would encounter harsh weather, deserts and raids by Native Americans as it began building west from Omaha. The work was hard, well-paying and steady for tens of thousands of laborers from across the country and around the world. The two railroads vigorously competed to lay the most track in the race to cover the 1,777 miles that separated them.

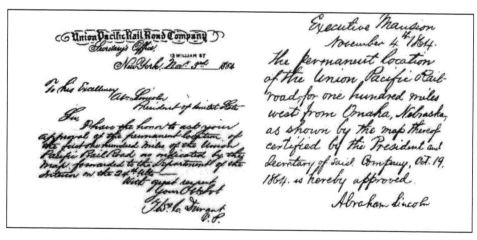

Abraham Lincoln's November 4, 1864 Approval Letter.

Pacific Railroad "Fever"

Transcontinental Railroad "fever" struck the Eastern States long before California joined the Union in 1850. The first proposals to gain a serious audience originated in 1845 with Asa Whitney, a New York merchant who had made a fortune in China trade. Until the gold rush and California's annexation, Congress considered most of these plans impractical. Northern and Southern traders disagreed about the railroad's route, further delaying action.

The Civil War Era

The Civil War sharpened Congressional fears of losing California through foreign intervention and increased the North's need for the gold and silver of the West. Meanwhile, Californians had become more eager to end the isolation from the rest of the nation. **The Pacific Railroad** symbolized their hopes for a better life, for new prosperity, and for unlimited expansion.

The times were intensely nationalistic and the visions of what the United States might encompass recognized no boundaries or limits. America's most ambitious leaders regarded Mexico, Canada and Asia as an advancement of trade. **The Transcontinental Railroad** would be a giant stride in this direction.

Chinese Immigrants – Ten Thousand Railroaders

Pushed from their homes by economic hardship and pulled to California by a shortage of labor, Chinese immigrants played a crucial role in building the Central Pacific. Young men had already begun immigrating from South China to California during the gold rush in 1849-50. **Charles Crocker**, in charge of **Central Pacific Construction**, lured the **first Chinese construction crew** because the railroad could not find enough Caucasian laborers. These crews showed such skill, reliability and perseverance that Central Pacific recruited thousands more Chinese workers in China itself. At the height of construction, over 10,000 Chinese men were at work on the Central Pacific.

Chinese Workers – Highly Motivated and Skilled

In the late 19th and early 20th centuries, there was a backlash against Asian immigration, and the real story of their involvement became clouded with myth and misinformation. These were highly motivated, and often skilled, workers who participated in the emerging American economy.

Hard Work and High Skill

Central Pacific's Chinese workers were highly skilled and motivated and comprised one of the most effective construction forces ever assembled. Skilled Chinese workers did most of the tunneling, drilling and blasting as the Central Pacific cut a path through the hard granite of the Sierra Nevada. The only way to remove rock was to drill a deep hole and pack it with black powder. Slow burning fuses ignited the powder, shattering the rock. Workers with shovels and carts removed the debris and shaped the rock by hand to its final profile. Often, they worked in brutal weather, and sometimes just getting access to the rock face to be drilled was difficult and dangerous. While these tasks involved only a small fraction of the Chinese workforce, and a few miles of track, they illustrate the skill and grit of the crews.

NO OTHER IMPROVEMENT ... CAN EQUAL IN UTILITY THE RAILROAD ABRAHAM LINCOLN MARCH 9 1832

On the wall of Union Station, Omaha, Nebraska.

The Last Spike, painting by Thomas Hill.
Courtesy of the California State Railroad Museum.
Pastor John Todd, Congregational minister from Massachusetts (in the foreground)
gave the Prayer to commence and ask God's blessing on the Last Spike celebration.

The Transcontinental Railroad was the last major American construction project completed before the introduction of better explosives, earthmoving machinery and modern construction techniques. All of the work was done by hand. Chinese workers joined the project soon after construction began at Sacramento in 1863, and they helped carry the last rail into place at Promontory, Utah, in May of 1869. After completion of the railroad, some workers returned to China; others settled in places like San Francisco and many moved to large construction projects elsewhere in the West. Many remained with the Central Pacific Railroad.

The Ten-mile Day
April 28, 1869

Near Promontory, Utah, a sign once stood marking April 28, 1869 when the Central Pacific laid ten miles of track in one day. Union Pacific Vice President, **Thomas Durant**, had wagered **Charles Crocker** that the Central Pacific could not out-do the Union Pacific's one-day record of seven miles. Crocker took the bet.

A select crew of Chinese and others set to work, directed by Construction Boss James Strobridge. They labored throughout the grueling, twelve-hour day, refusing to yield to a relief crew standing by. Working with military precision, they handled 25,800 ties, 3,520 rails, 55,000 pounds of spikes, 7,040 splice bars and 14,080 bolts – 4,362,000 pounds of material. When the men stopped work, **over ten miles of track lay in place**. The record set that day still stands.

Driving the Golden Spike
Promontory, Utah – May 10, 1869

Six years after the project began, one of the greatest engineering feats of the 19th century was ready for completion. On May 10th 1869, dignitaries, reporters, laborers and hundreds of onlookers gathered at Promontory, Utah to witness the driving of the golden spike, celebrating the completion of the Transcontinental Railroad. The event was instantly telegraphed to an eagerly waiting nation – America's first "live" media event.

Five days after completion, service began. A trip that once took months, now took only days. New towns and cities appeared, along with the people to fill them. Trains loaded with machinery and goods traveled west, and returned east loaded with agricultural products. The West was now fully open to settlement. To a nation with a modern, mechanized transportation system, anything seemed possible.

The "Lost" Spike

Until recently, very few people, historians included, were aware of a lost golden spike that was cast as part of the original order for the **Golden Last Spike of Transcontinental Railroad** fame. **In 1869**, San Francisco land developer, David

*Union Pacific and Central Pacific locomotives meet at
Promontory, Utah on May 10, 1849.*

*"The Governor Stanford" (CP No. 1) a 40-ton, wood-burning steam
locomotive, built in 1862, began service in Sacramento in 1863.*

Hewes, had **"THE" golden Last Spike** cast, hurriedly engraved, and sent with Leland Stanford to the ceremonies of Promontory. After the ceremony, the spike was returned to Hewes, who kept it for 23 years before donating it to Stanford University.

Until very recently, historians had assumed the words "Finishing two gold spikes" that appeared on the jeweler's invoice for the Last Spike, described polishing the sprue or extra metal attached to the spike during casting. We now know these words indicate David Hewes had two identical golden spikes cast at the same time. The first, the Last Spike, traveled to Promontory; the second, or "Lost Spike," remained with the Hewes family for well over a hundred years, its story untold.

While the two spikes are very similar, the engraving varies slightly between them. For instance, the Last Spike has the anticipated date of completion of the **Transcontinental Railroad** (May 8), not the actual date of May 10. Also, the quality of the engraving on the Last Spike has been described as "crude." This indicates the engraving was performed before the event and probably rushed for completion on time. The correct date and more delicate engraving on the "Lost Spike" indicate it was finished after the event, and not in a hurried manner.

The First Locomotive

The Central Pacific's first locomotive was a classic "American" type 4-4-0, typical of thousands of engines used throughout the United States. The newly-organized **Central Pacific Railroad** ordered a fleet of locomotives and cars. These were expensive and had to be purchased from the industrial centers of the East. The firm of *Richard Norris and Sons* in Philadelphia completed this locomotive in 1862. After an ocean journey around the tip of South America (Cape Horn), Number 1 arrived in Sacramento and made ready for work. Central Pacific honored its President (also the Governor of California), by naming the locomotive the "Governor Stanford." At first a wood burner, but later converted to burn coal, it could haul three coaches or ten freight cars over the steep grades through the Sierra Nevada. The first locomotive served for 3 decades.

The "Empire Builders"

"The Big Four" as they are called – Leland Stanford, Charles Crocker, Mark Hopkins and Collis P. Huntington used their considerable talents to accumulate wealth and power, and felt that hard work justified the rewards. Expanding their **Railroad Empire,** "The Big Four" built a transportation monopoly in California, made huge fortunes, and constructed elaborate San Francisco mansions to display their affluence.

Mark Hopkins – Oldest of the "Four" died in his sleep aboard a company train, nine years after completing the **First Transcontinental Railroad**.

Leland Stanford – Far exceeded his partners in generosity by endowing **Stanford University** in memory of his only child, who died in youth. The former **Governor**, elected to the United States Senate in 1885, died during his second term of office.

Charles Crocker – Continued to oversee Railroad construction, bought and sold property, and watched over work at the Del Monte Hotel in **Monterey,** where he died in 1888.

Collis P. Huntington – The last survivor, steadfastly ruled **the Company**. Acquisitive to the end, only a few years before his death in 1900, he attempted to delay the Railroad's repayment of its construction costs.

Conclusion

Who indeed, were the "**Four Pioneer Founders of California?**" – They came aboard the steamship *"California,"* arriving in Monterey on February 28, 1849, laying the foundations for the State, and paving the way during the Constitutional Convention for California's admission to the Union. From first-hand accounts, upon arrival on the Pacific Coast, San Francisco was a dismal place of tents, mud, shanties, gambling saloons, gold-seekers and pitiful conditions. Amid dire circumstances, obstacles, difficulties and setbacks, their steadfast faith, hard work, diligence, and trust in Almighty God, replaced the "gold-rush" with "God's rush to California." The names of these first Protestant pioneers – **Rev. Samuel Hopkins Willey, D.D.; Rev. Osgood Wheeler, D.D.; Rev. J.W. Douglas and Rev. Sylvester Woodbridge, Jr.** and their co-laborers – are engraved in stone and marble, a living testimony to God's Hand upon **California – America's First New England.**

To them belongs the honor of planting *Protestant Christianity* in California; of establishing the *First Free Public Schools*; the *First Newspapers*; the *First Libraries*; the *First College of California, Berkeley* – established "in the spirit of Christianity" – which became the University of California, Berkeley; the *First Sunday schools*; the *First Bible classes*; the *First Young Men's Christian Association*; the *First Bible Societies*, the first *Book and Tract Companies*, and many more "firsts."

They came as pioneer missionaries to California, then described as "the darkest mission field." They left an indelible mark of honesty, Christian values, and outreach – to **the Chinese**, in particular – but also to many other peoples and cultures drawn to California. Although highly educated, and erudite scholars in their own right, theirs was not a quest for "gold" – they wanted little of it – nor for affluence or power, but for the "gold which lasts and does not perish," the winning of souls for the Kingdom of Eternal Life.

California – The First New England – owes a great debt of gratitude to these **"Four Founders"** who laid down their lives in the founding and establishment of the 31st State – which can proudly trace its beginnings to June 17, 1579, when **Sir Francis Drake** celebrated the first Protestant Christian service in America. "He set up a great poste" accepting and claiming rightful ownership to the whole territory in the name of his sovereign, and dedicating it, "by the grace of God."

Endnotes

Preface

[1] First Hymn of the University of California, "Let There be Light." Jean Gray Hargrove Music Library, University of California, Berkeley.

Introduction

[1] Hunt, Rockwell D., Ph.D. *California Firsts*. San Francisco: Ferron Publishers, 1957.

Chapter IV

[1] Nimitz, Chester W. Fleet Admiral, USN, Honorary Chairman, Drake Navigators' Guild. Drake Luncheon Address, November 5,1962. *The Far Westerner*: Vol. 4, No. 1, January, 1963.

Chapter VI

[1] Phillips, D.L. *Letters from California*. Springfield: Illinois State Journal Co., 1877, p. 150

[2] Ibid., p. 151

[3] Ibid., p. 152

[4] Ibid.

[5] Wicher, Edward Arthur, D.D. *The Presbyterian Church in California – 1849-1927*. New York: Frederick H. Hitchcock, The Grafton Press,1927, p. 347.

[6] Ibid., p. 348

[7] Ibid.

[8] *California Historical Society Quarterly*, October, 1923.

[9] Wicher, Edward Arthur, D.D. *The Presbyterian Church in California – 1849-1927*. New York: Frederick H. Hitchcock, The Grafton Press,1927, p. 347.

[10] Carrere, John F., Maj. *Pioneer Religion in California,* 1923. Rare Manuscript Collection, California State Library, Sacramento, California.

[11] Ibid.

Chapter VII

[1] Willey, Samuel Hopkins, D.D., Chaplain of the Constitutional Convention. *Colton Hall Recollections,* Berkeley, California, May 31, 1904. To Hon. Joseph R. Knowland, Oakland, California (Typed manuscript of Rev. S.H. Willey)

[2] Willey, S.H., D.D. *Thirty Years in California – A Contribution to the History of the State from 1849-1879.* San Francisco: A.L. Bancroft & Co., Printers, 1879, p. 76.

[3] Hanchett, William. *The Question of Religion and the Taming of California* – The California Historical Society Quarterly, March, 1953, pp. 49, 50.

[4] Oakland Tribune, July 31, 1960. *Dartmouth Contribution.* Willey, S.H., (Rev., Pioneer, Congregational Minister).

[5] Phillips, D.L. *Letters from California.* Springfield: Illinois State Journal Co., 1877, p. 153.

[6] O'Brien, Robert. *First Steamship Pioneers,* Part I, February 28, 1949. Rare Manuscript Collection, California State Library, Sacramento California.

[7] Willey, Samuel Hopkins, D.D. *Hand-written letter.* Rare Manuscript Collection, California State Library, Sacramento, California.

[8] Ibid.

[9] Carrere, John F., Maj. *Pioneer Religion in California,* 1923. Rare Manuscript Collection, California State Library, Sacramento, California.

[10] *1849-1949 – One Hundred Golden Years for Christ.* Being a History of the First Baptist Church, San Francisco, California. San Francisco: First Baptist Church Publication, 1949, California.

[11] Ibid., pp. 8, 9.

[12] Carrere, John F., Maj. *Pioneer Religion in California*, 1923. Rare Manuscript Collection, California State Library, Sacramento, California.

[13] *California Historical Society Collection.* San Francisco, California.

[14] *Annual Directory, 1922. First Congregational Church*, Post and Mason Streets, San Francisco, California, p. 1.

[15] Ibid.

[16] Ibid., p. 2.

[17] Lampen, Michael D. *Grace Parish and Cathedral, 1849-1974.* An Historical Survey, 1974., p. 2. California Historical Society Collection.

[18] Ibid.

[19] Ibid.

[20] Carrere, John F., Maj. *Pioneer Religion in California*, 1923. Rare Manuscript Collection, California State Library, California.

[21] Lampen, Michael D. *Grace Parish and Cathedral, 1849-1974.* An Historical Survey, 1974, p. 3. California Historical Society Collection.

[22] Ibid.

[23] *San Francisco's Pioneer Congregations Celebration – 1849-1874.* California Historical Society Collection.

[24] Carrere, John F., Maj. *Pioneer Religion in California*, 1923. Rare Manuscript Collection, California State Library, Sacramento, California.

[25] *A History of the First Baptist Church, Sacramento, California, 1850-1950 – Centennial.* "Find One – Win One." In Commemoration of a Century for Christ, 1950, p. 8.

[26] Ibid., p. 11.

[27] Ibid., p. 9.

[28] Ibid., p. 36.

[29] Ibid., p. 37.

[30] Ibid., p. 39.

[31] Ibid.

[32] Carrere, John F., Maj. *Pioneer Religion in California*, 1923. Rare Manuscript Collection, California State Library, Sacramento, California.

[33] Ibid.

[34] Ibid.

[35] Ibid.

[36] Ibid.

[37] *Daily Alta California*, Vol. 1, No. 270, 28th October, 1850.

Chapter VIII

[1] Phillips, D.L. *Letters from California.* Springfield: Illinois State Journal Co., 1877, pp. 153, 154.

[2] Ibid., p. 154.

[3] Ibid., p. 155.

[4] Ibid., p. 156.

[5] Ibid.

[6] Ibid., p. 157.

Chapter IX

[1] *A Miner's Reverie.* Hutchings Illustrated California Magazine, Vol. II, July, 1857 – June, 1858. San Francisco: Hutchings and Rosenfield Publishers, 1858, pp. 34-36. Rare Manuscript Collection, California State Library, Sacramento, California.

[2] *California State Parks.* Coloma Library, California.

[3] Ibid.

[4] Ibid.

Chapter X

[1] Willey, S.H., D.D. Hand-written *Notebook,* 1888. Rare Manuscript Collection, Bancroft Library, University of California, Berkeley.

Chapter XI

[1] Willey, S.H., D.D. Hand-written *Vice-Regent's Report,* July, 1869. Rare Manuscript Collection, Bancroft Library, University of California, Berkeley.

[2] *Willey, S.H., D.D. to Baldwin, Theron, D.D.* Hand-written letter dated September 1, 1869. Rare Manuscript Collection, Bancroft Library, University of California, Berkeley.

Addendum

The Jodocus Hondius, circa 1595 Map:

The long Latin title merits full translation, as follows: "An accurate description of the voyage round the world of Sir Francis Drake, who set out from England with five well-equipped ships the 13th December 1577, circumnavigated the globe, and returned to England the 27th September 1580 with great glory but with one ship only, the others destroyed by fire and storms at sea. Also there is shown the voyage of another noble Englishman Thomas Cavendish who took the same course round the world but with less loss and in a shorter time, for he left on the 21st July 1586 and returned to his native Plymouth from whence he had set out on 15th September 1588. He acquired great riches and admiration of all his countrymen." The circumnavigations of both Drake and Cavendish are marked on the two hemispheres; between them at the top is the Elizabethan coat-of-arms and, below, a vignette of the famous *Golden Hinde*. Four corner vignettes show **Drake's landing at *Nova Albion*** in California, where Drake was crowned by the natives and their *Hioh* as king; and at ***"Portus Jave Majoris,"* island of *Java;*** Drake's welcome by the king of the Moluccas; and Drake's ship cast up on the rocks near the Celebes.

The name "Berkeley" – its origin and significance:

The name *"Berkeley"* for the new site of the College of California, was chosen by the Trustees of the College to honor George Berkeley, Bishop of Cloyne, and author of the phrase, *"Westward the course of empire takes its way."* The city was laid out in 1864 and in 1866 was given its name - *"Berkeley."*

The Seal and Motto of the University of California – Its Design and Symbolism:

...What special devices, what chosen emblems, appear upon the Seal of the University of California, and what is their significance? The symbols are few, yet admirable in their distinguished simplicity and in their striking appropriateness; their import, too, being both commendable and inspiring. Upon a ground of azure blue, denoting Loyalty and Truth, is emblazoned the Golden Book of Knowledge and Wisdom, with pages opened wide to intimate that its treasures are not reserved for the favored few, but are freely offered to all who can and will "read, mark, learn and inwardly digest." Above this noble device, emblematic of the work of the University, is the Morning Star, scattering its effulgent Rays of Inspiration upon the open Book, bathing it, as it were, with celestial glory and encircling it as with a halo of Dignity and Heavenly Benediction. And below, upon the Scroll, are the *imperishable words* which, uttered by the ***Divine Author and Architect of the***

Universe Himself, preceded the first stupendous **act of Creation**: **"Let There Be Light."** A motto which none could be more noble or more fitting. (Being Talk No. 10 of the Series, to be broadcast over Radio K.P.O., from the Studio on the Campus at Berkeley, on Monday, April 25, 1932, at 9:45 a.m. by Leonard Wilson, Instructor in Genealogy, Heraldry & Family Nomenclature, University of California).

The Bancroft Library
University of California, Berkeley:

The Bancroft Library is the primary special collections library at the University of California, Berkeley. It is one of the largest and most widely used libraries of manuscripts, rare books and unique materials in the United States. When it was acquired by the University in 1906 from publisher and bookseller, **Hubert Howe Bancroft**, its 50,000 volumes on the history of California and the American West made it the largest library in the country devoted to a single region – which is still the case today. Its holdings, as of 2010, include more than 600,000 manuscript items; 8,000,000 photographs and other pictorial materials, 43,000 microforms and 23,000 maps. **Hubert Howe Bancroft (1832-1918)** – Bancroft's life has been defined by two compelling passions – books and history – which inspired a remarkable life. He was a "literary industrialist" – bookseller, publisher, historian, author and editor – who built the collection that is at the heart of the Library. A natural student – he could read by the age of three. Bancroft gained a wide knowledge of languages and classical authors from whom he quoted prodigiously throughout his writings. He was highly successful in the "literary industries" of publishing, editing and selling books at a time when San Francisco was first booming. He was then able to pursue his great desire by building a landmark library that laid the foundations for a monumental history of the American West, and a research library unique in the world. **Bancroft** contrasts his *Puritan forebears' "pilgrimage"* to Ohio in the early 19th century with the fevered gold-seekers "exodus" to California a few years later. *"Quite a contrast to that which characterized the exodus to California less than half a century later, wherein greed usurped the place of godliness, lust the place of love...Sacrifice, there was enough of it, but of quite a different kind. Comfort, society with its wholesome restraints, and Sabbath were sacrificed; the Bible, the teachings of their youth, and Christ Himself were sacrificed...drunken revelry and gambling took the place of Psalms and Sermons...Here was a new departure in colonizing; nor yet a colonizing – only a building of humanity, drunk from excess of avarice."* **In 1856, aged 24** and bearing a $5,000 loan from his sister, **Bancroft** returned to San Francisco for good, a place in which he perceived practically limitless possibilities: *"...I found myself in the year of 1856 in the newly Americanized and gold-burnished country of California, in the city of San Francisco...beside a bay unequalled by any along the whole 7,000-mile of shoreline, and unsurpassed a harbor by any in the world. Young, strong, with untouched, un-*

dreamed-of resources a thousand-fold more dazzling than any yet uncovered, with a million matchless years before her during which to turn, and overturn the world's great civilization, penetrate the mysteries of time, and bring to pass the unknowable..."

In his **"Literary Industries"** Bancroft describes his Market Street, San Francisco Library as, "...a room equivalent to 35 by 170 feet, being about 50 feet wide at the south end and narrowing irregularly toward the north end. The ceiling was low, and the view broken by the enclosures under the skylights, and by sections of standing supports with which it was found necessary to supplement the half mile and more of shelving against the walls...Yet all through the dozen years that the library was there, I trembled for its safety through fear of fire as indeed did many others who appreciated its historical significance to this coast, well knowing that once lost, no power on earth could reproduce it."

ABOUT THE AUTHOR

Catherine Millard, B.A., M.A., D. Min., has been a scholar and researcher at the Library of Congress of the United States for the past 22 years. She has also studied at the Hebrew University of Jerusalem.

Dr. Millard is president of *Christian Heritage Tours, Inc.*® and *Christian Heritage Ministries.*® She is the recipient of the George Washington Honor Medal, sponsored by the Freedoms Foundation at Valley Forge, and the Faith and Freedom, Religious Heritage of America Award. She has also been elected to "Who's Who Among Students in American Colleges and Universities" for outstanding academic achievement.

She is the author of eleven historical books, eight of which are on the original history and heritage of America.

Dr. Millard has lectured and taught extensively in colleges, universities and schools throughout the United States, and abroad.

Catherine Millard is also available to provide teaching seminars, lectures and multimedia presentations to your school or organization, on the subject of California's – and the nation's – original Christian heritage and history. You may contact her through the following address:

Christian Heritage Ministries®
P.O. Box 797,
Springfield, Virginia 22150
United States of America

Telephone: 703-455-0333
www.christianheritagetours.org
www.christianheritagemins.org

Additional copies of this book are available through the above address.